REPUBLIC OF SIGNS

Anne Norton

Republic of Signs

Liberal Theory

and American

Popular Culture

The University of Chicago Press
Chicago and London

ANNE NORTON is professor of political science at the University of Pennsylvania.

The University of Chicago Press, Chicago 60637
The University of Chicago Press, Ltd., London
© 1993 by The University of Chicago
All rights reserved. Published 1993
Printed in the United States of America
02 01 00 99 98 97 96 95 94 93   5 4 3 2 1

ISBN (cloth): 0-226-59512-9
ISBN (paper): 0-226-59513-7

Library of Congress Cataloging-in-Publication Data

Norton, Anne.
    Republic of signs: liberal theory and American popular culture / Anne Norton.
        p.   cm.
    Includes bibliographical references and index.
    ISBN 0-226-59512-9 (cloth).—ISBN 0-226-59513-7 (paper)
        1. Liberalism—United States.   2. Political culture—United States.   3. Representative government and representation—United States.   4. United States—Popular culture.   I. Title.
    JA84.U5N58   1993
    320.5'1'0973—dc20   92-36749
                                                                    CIP

⊗ The paper used in this publication meets the minimum requirements of the American National Standard for Information Sciences—Permanence of Paper for Printed Library Materials, ANSI Z39.48-1984.

CONTENTS

THIS BOOK IS A DIVERSION. In writing it, I was diverted (or so it seemed to me then) from the former course of my research. Andrew Ross, with whom I once taught, taught me to look into popular culture. Partisans and critics of liberalism Bruce Ackerman, Bill Connolly, Jim Fishkin, Dick Flathman, Bonnie Honig, Ira Katznelson, Uday Mehta, Carole Pateman, Alan Ryan, Joan Scott, and Rogers Smith made me see the importance of their debates. Sotirios Barber, Will Harris, Ellen Kennedy, Sandy Levinson, Walter Murphy, Kim Scheppele, and Jeffrey Tulis showed me that the Constitution was a constitution. That was a revelation.

This book was a diversion in still another sense. It was amusing to write. I enjoyed it, people enjoyed looking at pop culture with me, and I have hopes that readers will enjoy it as well. Graduate and undergraduate students at Princeton and the University of Texas read their clothes, brought me comic books, fotonovellas, and ads and cassettes, and continually reminded me of why pop culture is fascinating. Parts of this book were presented in various forms at many seminars and conferences. The most valuable conversations I had with my colleagues (inside and outside the university) commonly occurred informally. Ari and Vera Zolberg sent me a Barbara Kruger shopping bag emblazoned with the eminently appropriate slogan "I shop therefore I am" and left their mark on my thinking about the uses of art. Early on, Victoria Hattam made the encouraging observation that the account of consumption made her want to buy something. She has talked with me about many aspects of popular culture since. I have had, perhaps, the most intelligent company that any woman ever shopped with: Jim Henson, Gretchen Ritter, Lloyd and Susanne Rudolph, Helene Silverberg, Kaja Silverman, and Sheldon Wolin among them. I've eaten and argued with Thomas Dumm, Jennifer Hochschild, Richard Merelman, Michael Rogin, Diane Rubenstein, Jim Scott, George Shulman, Paul Smith, Tracy Strong, and Tamara Waggener. As I was writing this book, I was brought into moments of African-American culture and concerns. A part of America opened to me, and I owe Raphael Allen, Leslie Fields, Michael Hanchard, Nancy Tartt, Wahneema Lubiano, Valerie Smith, and Cornel West special thanks for that. The epilogue, and the first chapter, owe much to conversations with Bill Bradley. Deborah Harrold and Maureen Pickart McClure have supplied commentaries on popular culture and American practices since we came to school together. We were taught that "the unexamined life is not worth living."

THE FORCE OF A POLITICAL IDEA lies in its capacity to transcend thought and make itself part of everyday life in the material world. Liberalism has become the common sense of the American people, a set of principles unconsciously adhered to, a set of conventions so deeply held that they appear (when they appear at all) to be no more than common sense. The capacity of liberalism to transform itself in America from ideology to common sense is the proof—as it is the means—of its constitutional power.

This is a study of the enactment of liberal ideas in popular culture, in the possessions of ordinary people, in the habits of everyday life. Ideas are most powerful not when they impose practices upon us but when we take them for granted, not when their primacy is aggressively asserted but when they go unquestioned. Instances of liberal theory made manifest and material in the commonplace are evidence of that theory's profound success in constituting a form of life. The power of liberal ideas has extended beyond the ideal to the material, beyond thought to practice, beyond reason to habit. Popular practice has become liberalism's quotidian incarnation.

Those artifacts, aspects, and practices of popular culture that figure here were chosen because they illustrate the operation of some aspect of liberal theory in everyday life. They are a diverse lot. They include the *National Enquirer* and the work of Larry Rivers, the practices of voting, shopping, survey research, and the lottery. The practices considered here are neither peculiar to a single class nor common to us all. The artifacts, though common enough, are not common to all. There is

no single everyday life. The conduct of life is the practical realization of difference. Individual practices, and the individual
experience of collective identity in everyday life, mark us out
from one another and make the quotidian impenetrably singular. Yet the constitution and expression of a private identity depend upon the use of languages accessible to all. The practices
of everyday life oscillate between this impenetrable singularity
and our community in language, confirming both.

Political theorists commonly avoid examining their everyday lives, moved more by the dismissive Socratic observation
that matters of mud and hair are beneath the philosopher, than
by the maxim that "the unexamined life is not worth living."
Yet our practices, like those of our compatriots, silently insist
that we read what is written in dress, in commodities, in eating,
and in a plethora of other quotidian activities. There is much to
be discovered in these cultural practices. Neither theory nor
politics has kept to the boundaries scholars have set for it. The
practices and artifacts of everyday life are not merely things to
be explained. They contain commentaries on the theories and
the principles they enact.

The practices that indicate most forcefully, most perva-
sively, the translation of liberal principles into common practice
offer practical examinations of those principles. As they cast
thought into practice, they present commentaries on the theories in which they are embedded. In doing so, certain of those
practices offer critiques of the principles they realize. The practices of liberalism make liberals liberalism's practical critics.

Common sense and the wisdom of experience have long
argued that theories must be distrusted until they are proven in
practice, for the conditions of everyday life differ from the conditions of thought. The movement from principle to practice,
from the theoretical to the popular, from thought to material
things alters what it enacts. The enactment of constitutional
principles and constitutive ideas reveals unlooked-for applica-
tions and limitations. In enactment the full import of these principles becomes visible and intelligible. Yet principles change as
they are enacted, in the ends they are thought to serve or the
costs they are thought to entail. As they do their work, directing
the constitution of their world, they change their context. With
that they change their meaning, and their consequences. They

are changed by what they change. Mundane demands place new limits—and reveal new possibilities—as thought becomes real in the world. The enactment of the principles of representative government in America has subjected these principles to the revelatory demands of everyday life. Representation is not merely a form of governance, it is also the means we use to create ourselves in a new world order. The American reliance on representation as a form of authority extends beyond political institutions and into popular practices. Americans give the nation written form in the Constitution. They give themselves a written form in practice. The people separately enact the national transubstantiation, moving from word to flesh in living as the constituted nation, moving from flesh to word in the individual creation of literary selves. Americans represent themselves in public documents and private letters, diplomas and diaries. In education, institutions, and the mundane practices of everyday life, Americans read and write themselves (as they read and write their nation) into being.

This self-conscious being in language does not replace being in the flesh. The constraints of the body are partially evaded, but the needs and desires of the body are enhanced and elaborated in writing and in these written selves. These are selves of our own making, subject, like ourselves, to the constraints of word and flesh, composed, like ourselves, in languages and social orders not of our making. There are no selves more real, no selves more authentic, than these.

The selves of liberal practice are not the selves of liberal theory. Convinced, in theory, of our individuality, we find ourselves in common languages and express ourselves (even rebel) in conformity with existing conventions. Convinced, in theory, of our singularity, we exceed ourselves, supplementing the form we inhabited at birth with an array of literary selves not always in accord with one another. Convinced, in theory, of our unity, we deconstruct ourselves in practice, giving ourselves material expression in collections of diverse commodities. Convinced, in theory, that the unity of the self is necessary to happiness and perhaps to sanity, we experience this deconstructive enterprise not only as a source of anxiety but also as an act of authority and a source of pleasure.

The second chapter explores this aspect of our national preoccupation with representation. The diverse and often sophisticated ways in which Americans use consumption as a means of representation reveal the governing presence of the political in the (only) nominally private realm. Commodities, particularly clothing, provide a lexicon for the signification of a variety of traits: gender, class, and regional identity, occupation, avocation, politics, and sexual preference. Americans employ this lexicon self-consciously. This consciousness of consumption as a form of speech underlies the insistence on the availability of consumer goods as an index of political freedom. The use of commodities as a means for the expression of individuality gives us another language and other material forms. Our use of this language in goods is not merely a form of self-expression, the practice of an already constituted self. It is a constitutional practice—in which we make ourselves. In this, as in other languages, we find ourselves in forms that were there before us, and we alter them, where we will and where we can, to our specifications.

The practice of shopping enacts liberal theory's identification of choice with freedom and, in that enactment, suggests a critique. Individuality, the conventions governing property, and the utility of representation as an instrument for the expression of the author's will are all called into question. We realize, as we shop, that choice may be experienced as freedom, and as compulsion. The choices we appear to make have already been made for us. The individuality we prize is realized in purchases that deconstruct it. Property shows itself not only as a means for self-protection, self-expression, and self-discovery but also as a means for subjecting us to the authority of others. The enactment of the ideas of liberalism works simultaneously to confirm and to subvert them.

The ambivalent practices of popular culture inform our institutional practices as well. The third chapter pursues Tocqueville's recognition of the President as sign. The presidency is a complex economy of representations, authority and subjection, sight and secrecy. Succession makes each subsequent President the author of those who came before, but it invests this President with an office whose meaning was authored by predecessors. Presidents acquire authority over the office, their predecessors, and history through a process marked by their subjection. The candidate is constructed as commodity, product, and text, subject to the authority of others.

The instances of language that made themselves visible in popular culture—the language of commodities, the texts written in the image—show themselves here as well. In this chapter the politics of sight, already visible in the use of commodities as a language, shows itself at work in institutions. The visible singularity of the President advantages both the presidency and particular Presidents, for it makes the President a readily accessible sign for a single united people. The authority sight vests in Presidents, the authority denied candidates seen as commodities, the silent texts that can be read in campaign advertisements and press conferences are all seen but not heard, read but rarely spoken of, for we have maintained silence, in popular culture as in the academy, about what speaks in the image. We are in practice, as we are in our Constitution, people of the text.

Each of the first three chapters shows Americans constituting themselves, as individuals and partisans, through representation. The fourth chapter, "Our Homeland the Text," looks to the canonical locus of this constitution through representation: the Constitution. In this chapter I look at the recognition, in the Constitution, of the dialectical relation of text and people, word and flesh. Recognition of this dialectic leads to a clearer understanding of the connection between representation (particularly the fictions of representation), transcendence, and the realization of national aspirations.

The fifth chapter concerns the presence of Americans before the law. Lawyers and the law occupy prominent positions in American politics and history. The law, lawyers, judges, police officers, and detectives occupy prominent positions in American popular culture. In politics and popular culture, Americans meet the law with veneration and indifference, lawyers with respect and contempt. This ambivalence is altogether appropriate to a people who believe that they stand before the law in both senses: subject to the law's rule, and prior to it in time and authority. The practices of the law show another ambivalence as well, that between the spoken and the written word.

The final chapter discusses the tensions between words and

images, speech and silence. Many of the structures of American politics—the form of the trial, electoral campaigns, the language of commodities—acknowledge in practice the tensions and disparities in these diverse forms of representation. This chapter is directed against the presumption of the neutrality of language. Liberal theorists have ignored the visual texts—the meanings race and gender inscribe on the bodies of speakers, their arrangement in a room, their representation on television—that inflect the speeches we hear. The assertion—even the strict maintenance—of freedom of speech does not entirely overcome the disparate costs entailed on speeches with different contents and contexts.

This book is thus an examination of the practices of a people who govern themselves through representation. Those practices that come under the rubric of representation, whether semiotic or political, invariably seem to provide instances of supplementarity, that which "adds, only to replace." [1] Writing presents itself as a mere supplement to—a representation of—speech, yet writing replaces speech in the constitution of those who use (and therefore live in) language. Nevertheless, speech remains, remade by writing. The many mechanisms of political representation present themselves in the theory of liberalism as instruments for the refinement and expression of popular will, the consent of the people. In liberal practice, representation has served to silence the will and replace consent. Still, the will remains, shaped by representation, instructed in the limits of choice and consent.

Political representation is not the only instance of supplementarity in the practices of liberalism. Visual images, which are often presented—on television, in advertising—as mere illustrations of a verbal text, provide a legible, intelligible text that may replace, and will inevitably inflect, the verbal text it seems to supplement. Consider too the language of commodities. Any commodity may serve as a signifier of identity, status, and allegiance. It presents itself as a mere representation of the position it signifies, no more. Yet often the signifier acquires the independence of currency, functioning as if it had value in itself. We see this in the domestication of ethnicity and the transformation of the marks of difference into commodities.

Supplementarity, like representation, is duplicitous. That

which acts as a supplement adds and subtracts, opens and closes. The change the supplement evokes opens the possibility of transcendence: of the material, of our collective defects. Yet it may close off history. The constitutional text, with its evocation of a more perfect union, is silent on the present condition and the history of the nation. The belief in a common individuality extends the promise of equality before the law, but this equality is subverted in the construction of race and gender as supplements to a universal individuality, entailing a covert acknowledgment of "the individual" as white and male.

The operation of the supplement should not, however, be mistaken for the "original sin" of postmodernity, or representation as the liberal Fall. Representation, in its lack of transparency, in its excess and inadequacy, in its duplicities, also makes possible the escapes, escapades, and transcendent dignity of civilization. The lie written in representation makes possible escape from some of the determinative effects of language; its aporetic character enables one to enhance (where one cannot escape) a series of material constitutions. Political representation is similarly marked by the virtues and defects of this duplicity. The duplicities made possible in written constitutions enable peoples to become themselves, to constitute an ideal nationality that will overcome the defects and failings of their constitution in the present material world.

The principles, assumptions, and categories of liberalism, and the enactment of these in the practices of a liberal people, are separated by a considerable distance, but this is not the distance between principle and hypocrisy or aspiration and inadequacy. It is the distance that separates a form of life from its overcoming of itself.

Liberalism has overcome itself in its realization in popular culture. This practical self-overcoming should be recognized (that is, acknowledged and rethought) by both its critics and its partisans. Critics must acknowledge the power of liberalism to constitute a way of life, and credit liberalism with the achievement of the revaluations that will be—as such revaluations inevitably are—its own undoing. Liberals must acknowledge that the success of their constitutional enterprise has created liberals who have realized the limits of liberalism.

ONE

Republic of Signs

BROUGHT FORTH BY A DECLARATION, constituted in writing, Americans place themselves under the authority of language. The Declaration spoke the nation into being. The Constitution stands not as an artifact, or as mere law, but as the written representation of America. The establishment of republican government in America secured not simply representative government but a regime in which representation itself has primacy.

The Constitution represents a collective, conscious, willful entry into the symbolic order. In it Americans become a people of the text. The founders of the regime, and their posterity, mark the Constitution as the creation of a new world order, *novus ordo seclorum*. Mindful of the authority of language over them, Americans seize that authority for themselves. They exchange a natural for a scriptural constitution and in so doing undertake to fashion a world order that in its rationality, its breadth, and its justice would surpass that of the God of Nature.

Literary Selves

In this new, and literary, world order each moment of individual life is carefully inscribed. Births are recorded, names chosen, and birth certificates issued. The child is registered for school and by the census. Attendance is recorded, grades assigned. There are school files, medical files, perhaps a file at the FBI. One acquires a social security number, perhaps a passport, perhaps some visas, a voter's registration card, a draft registration card, a driver's license, innumerable identity cards. Each card invokes an identity. One can be a student, a member of the armed forces, an employee, a member of a museum, a "card-carrying Communist," or, for that matter, "a card-carrying member of the ACLU." As the expression *card-carrying* implies, possession of cards, certificates, and diplomas gives greater reality to elements of one's identity. They are taken as currency for qualifications and beliefs.

Without a name, without identification, one does not exist for the various agencies of government. If one does not produce a voter registration card, or appear by name, in writing, on the registration rolls, one is not permitted to vote. Without a diploma one cannot practice law or medicine. It will not do to produce one's mother to testify to the conditions of one's birth; a birth certificate is required. Without a name, without cards and forms and writings, citizens scarcely exist, either for the government or for one another.

The exchange of a literary for a corporeal identity marks the exchange of the old world for the new. Under the ancien régime one was born into one's place. Family ties determined not only one's place but the understanding one had of oneself. Much of this remains. Yet in the new world, one could overcome the conditions of one's birth. One could remake oneself in writing.

Lincoln, who rose from poverty to preeminence, is perhaps the most-renowned example of the literary reconstruction of the self. When asked of his past, he said that he preferred to leave it in unwritten obscurity. Through reading and the practice of the law, through writing and election, he remade himself. After his death, in history and biography, speeches and the carved words of the Lincoln Memorial, he was again remade. He exists for us still in speech and writing, though he is long since dead as a man.

In becoming a people of the text, themselves inscribed, the Jews found a collective scriptural transcendence. The Christians promised an individual transcendence, secured by the scriptural promise of inclusion in the resurrection of the deity. The common practices of the American regime similarly attempt to secure a scriptural transcendence to us all. No life goes unrecorded here. Records of individual births and deaths, of taxes and social security payments and military service, fill the archives. Like the Mormons, that most American of churches, historians and archaeologists attempt to recover those whose lives went unrecorded, that they too will be remembered and numbered among us.

The formal constitution of written identity in records, documents, and archives is accompanied by less formal constitutions of a literary self. We make ourselves from the materials of books and films, television and popular music, newspapers and magazines. We inscribe ourselves upon the world singly and collectively: in letters, diaries, yearbooks, notes, and papers. Citizens constitute themselves as voters and petitioners and as instances of already written categories: Democrat and Republican, liberal and conservative, male and female, black and white. We rely on writing to represent ourselves to the state and to one another.

The privileging of this written over a more corporeal identity permits individuals to extend themselves beyond their temporal boundaries in their imaginations and their rule. We accept Washington, Lincoln, Walt Whitman, and Martin Luther King, Jr., Jefferson and Geronimo, slaves and immigrants, outlaws and frontiersmen as our compatriots. These people, who we never knew in the flesh, are present in our words and thoughts. We cite them in political debates and bring them to mind in our considerations of American nationality. We accept, in our acceptance of their nation as our own, kinship to a posterity we will never see, a duty to people not yet born.

It is not, however, only the boundary between the quick and the dead that lapses in the ascendance of the literary self. The boundary between the embodied and the incorporate lapses as well. Corporations are institutionally and informally ascribed independent identity. Advertising and ordinary conversations as well as the law personify them. People spoke of "Ma Bell"; employees refer to their firms as "Arthur" and "Leo." They ascribe not only interests but traits and values to

11

them. These are not the only fictive persons we acknowledge. We know certain creations of high and popular culture—Ahab, Scrooge, Huck Finn, Jay Gatsby, the Jetsons, Ralph Kramden, Archie Bunker, J. R. Ewing, Pee Wee Herman, and Miss Piggy—better than we know our neighbors. We know their occupations, histories, and attributes. We discuss their business ventures and family scandals. We tell anecdotes about them. We cite their opinions in our political discourse.

This startling confabulation of the quick and the dead, the two- and the three-dimensional, is often read as evidence of an incapacity in the American mind, another element in a much-lamented decline. The American horror of aristocratic distinction has produced citizens lacking not only in taste but in more fundamental modes of discrimination, unable to discern the boundaries between themselves and their creations. There is a sense, of course, in which this is nonsense. The "average American" who opened the door to Fred Flintstone would be very surprised indeed. No one expected to see Clark Kent's byline in the evening paper, or J. R. Ewing at a meeting of oilmen. What we see in the American acceptance of these fictive persons—in certain contexts, and for certain purposes—is not a decline into ignorance but an increase in sophistication.

The inclusion of fictive persons in conversation as in law bears witness to the popular recognition that persons, and personality, are social constructions. Americans, in such acts, take the literary self for granted. They assume it and in this assumption acknowledge that those who participate in the political, economic, and social life of our culture do so in character, in roles defined without their full knowledge or consent, with personalities, interests, and ends that they develop and express through representation. They recognize that they—and all others—figure in the political order not in their natural but in their literary constitutions. In acknowledging the creations of popular culture as their compatriots, they know themselves to be a people constituted in language, whose homeland is the text.[1]

This construction of themselves as people of the text makes the charge that Americans mistake their creations for themselves not altogether nonsensical. The regime makes them their own creation. Collectively, they author their common constitu-

12

tion. They are, in their singularity, the authors of their private constitutions.

Making History

The institutions of representative government, and the establishment of written constitutions for nations and their citizens, are not peculiar to the United States. They are common, if not to all the world, at least to the postindustrial societies of Western Europe. Europeans, however, continue to regard this kinship with unease. Aspects of the passion for representation are still presented by European intellectuals as conditions peculiar to America.

The creation of a new world order manifests itself materially in American culture, particularly American popular culture, in what Umberto Eco describes as a "furious hyperreality." In his essay *Travels in Hyperreality*, Eco observes the American passion for representation. He describes a variety of American reproductions—of presidential offices, drawing rooms of deceased bourgeois families, founders, nature, and fictive futures.

Lyndon Johnson's reconstructions of the Oval Office, the diorama of Peter Stuyvesant, the reconstruction of the 1906 drawing room of Mr. and Mrs. Harkness Flagler all testify, in Eco's view, to an American passion for the making (and unmaking) of history. There is, he suggests, "a constant in the average American imagination and taste, for which the past must be preserved and celebrated in full-scale, authentic copy." [2] Americans are inevitably defeated in their Egyptian impulse to preserve a past that time has a prior claim to. Their remakings of the past unmake it, for in them " 'the completely real' becomes identified with 'the completely fake.' " The past, Eco observes, is unmade in its reconstruction. The simulacrum "assumes the aspect of a reincarnation." The past is overcome, for the reproduction does not merely recall but replaces it. [3]

Eco reads in these American reproductions a rejection of history, of the construction of the past as past, of the nation as temporal. Americans willfully construct the past as present. They remove artifacts from their exhibition cases, then remove from these the evidence of age, disuse, and decay, they attempt to rejoin objects separated from one another, they reassemble fragments.

The reconstruction of period rooms in the Metropolitan, of the Oval Office in the LBJ Library, or of Main Street in Disneyland is predicated on assumptions, and on an end, altogether different from those that inform the European tradition of museums. It is not an attempt to preserve the residue of a lost material culture, whether in sentimental remembrance or a pious and awful veneration of the past. It is an attempt to recall a context. In it we affirm that the past is present to us or, more accurately, that the past is absent. There is only the present. Histories and museums, artifacts and reconstructions, are all appropriations.

Europeans, Nietzsche writes, comprehend history as a collection of artifacts, fragmentary and alien. Their museums manifest their inner life. Their knowledge of the past rattles about in them like a collection of stones that they cannot digest.[4] They can neither make it their own nor rid themselves of it, yet it weighs heavily with them.

Eco is in thrall, as Walter Benjamin was before him, to the concept of "authenticity," and the presumptions about history inscribed within it. Benjamin writes, "The presence of the original is the prerequisite to the concept of authenticity," and supplies an example of how this presence is to be understood. "Chemical analysis of the patina of bronze can help to establish this."[5] The physical form of the object is venerated as the horizon and the prison of its presence. History is carried in the patina.

The object is absurdly inflated, and sadly diminished, in this idolatry. No object is quite large enough to carry its history within it. Something of the past, of the place and uses of the object, even something of its meaning, may be read, scientifically, hermeneutically, in its material composition, but this reading of the object's mass does not exhaust it. Objects exceed themselves practically, semiotically, temporally. They are not confined to the limits of their physical form in their meaning or their effects. They become less—and more—meaningful in the absence of their past context, more, and differently, meaningful in the acquisition of another. They are given meaning by contexts the object's physical form cannot give access to.

The belief that in possessing an object we possess its history, its meaning, its full significance, and that these, inhering in the object's physical form, are ours alone, is the faith of the collector. This is the mentality that prefers a single first edition to a set of an admired author's works. For those who follow **15** Benjamin, the "authentic" American Constitution rests in a case somewhere, a text for collectors, a museum piece.

The simultaneous affirmation of the absence of history and the presence of the past is at the foundation of the American regime. It is written into the Constitution, where we, the people, speak out of time, equally present in present, past, and future. Those who read the Preamble speak as their predecessors did, as sovereign. No difference is admitted between them. When Americans celebrated the bicentennial of this document, there were copies of the Constitution in Constitutional Hall and in neighborhood schools and groceries for one to sign or not sign, as one chose. Whether one aligned oneself with the Federalists or the Anti-Federalists—or, for that matter, with the indolent or the indifferent—one stood with the generation of the founding.

It may be that "to speak of things that one wants to connote as real these things must seem real," but this does not mean that "the 'completely real' becomes identified with the 'completely fake.' " The American who signs (or refuses to sign) the Constitution in the grocery knows that the signatures, unlike those to the "completely real" document of 1787, are not those of delegates to a constitutional convention. Yet the signature in the grocery, and the assent it signifies, legitimates as those preserved in the archives cannot. The later Constitution is not "completely fake," for the first was not "completely real." The Constitution has been realized in the years since 1787.

In their bicentennial celebrations of the Constitution, Americans acted in accordance with an ideology that denies the determinative power of history. The construction of the Constitution as a document to be immediately confronted, whose legitimacy was always and everywhere in question, subject to continual consideration, requiring the constant consent of the people, confirmed it as the Constitution.

American constructions of the Oval Office and the opening of the offices of mayors, governors, and Presidents to tourists are also ideologically inflected. It is necessary, in America, that the White House be open to tourists, that any American can walk into the Oval Office and stand in the place of the President. It is a rare child (perhaps, a rare adult) who does not walk over and sit in the President's chair.

This action, and others that resemble it, carry a many-layered message. Those who do this stand in the place of authority. Their capacity to occupy this place is affirmed. It is marked as open to them. They are told not simply that "any child may grow up to be President" (though this hoary and improbable declaration has a well-established place in American myth) but that, in an attenuated and figurative, but nevertheless present, sense, they stand in the place of the President. They occupy the centers of authority. In such actions they become participants in the representation of their collective sovereignty. That these, like all other representations, are fictions does not deprive them of significance. They remain constitutive of the ideal, if not the actual, forms of the American regime.

The play with these trappings of authority also tends to divest them of the power to legitimate by evocation. If anyone can sit in a chair, or stand behind a podium with a seal, and have their picture taken with a Polaroid, possession of that chair or that seal carries less with it. The practice of opening the places and distributing the objects that signify authority at once diffuses that authority and makes it necessary to obtain legitimation through other means. This form of play prevents, in this instance, the signifiers of authority from displacing the processes of legitimation they signify.

The creation of places from the past and future is similarly imbued with ideological importance. The period rooms in the Metropolitan, Disneyland's Main Street, and the Wild West sections of innumerable theme parks, Tomorrowland, and Epcot Center make the past and the future similarly accessible. In these, Americans ascribe to themselves the capacity to transcend time. They do so not, as it first appears, by pretending to a perfect access to the past but rather through an acknowledgment of history as fiction.

The recollection of the past in period rooms and theme parks is clearly marked, and experienced, as a construction. These places are inside a gate, past the ticket taker, within sight of contemporary structures and artifacts, in the presence of the present. Those who enter these worlds cannot escape the recognition that they enter a history of their own making. They are architecturally instructed in the embeddedness of history in the present.

17

The custom of maintaining artifacts unrestored, without repair, has an ideology of its own. It purports to preserve the historical authenticity of the objects displayed by minimizing the action of the present upon them. But it is not the hand of the restorationist, or the addition of modern materials in repair, that attaches the present to the past. This activity is accomplished more completely, and less obtrusively, by context and in the action of the mind. The material repair and restoration of these objects merely gives material expression, material form, to the ideal reconstruction of the past by the present.

Dirt, mud, and tarnish, frayed edges, and rotted cloth serve as signifiers of an object's age. More than this, they signify the material reality of history. They suggest that the object we have in the present is the same object that existed in the past, and that in it we confront the past without the mediation of the present. This is not so. Objects are constructed out of matter and in the mind. They are invested not only with a material form but with a social place, a use, a context, and all the meanings that attach to these. The possession of the object in its material form gives no perfect access to these.

The preservation of an object with all the marks of age upon it might serve as a reminder that the ideal losses and accretions it has suffered are no less damaging. The placement of such objects in display cases, out of any context but that of the gallery or museum, might bring to mind the dismembering preservation of the past that Nietzsche ridicules. More often, however, these actions serve to disguise the reconstitution of the past in the present. The tender preservation of these material forms invests them with independent importance. The attribution of "authenticity" permits their possessors to claim that in them they possess the past. Together these practices construct the historical past as having an altogether material constitution. They draw our minds away from a consciousness of their own constitutive power.

The presence, throughout America, of diverse renderings of the Old West, the Old South, Colonial America, and the Republic of Texas makes the role of interpretation in the writing of history equally conspicuous. Apprised of the constructed character of history, Americans are also instructed in the availability of different versions of the past. They see history not as the past but as diverse readings of the past. They see it made again in the present.

The historical paintings of Larry Rivers express a similar consciousness of the making of history. *Webster* reveals history as a re-presentation, multiplying the image of the senator, each time altering the image. His *History of the Russian Revolution* presents history as a construct. The smooth historical paintings of Jacques-Louis David and John Trumbull likewise present themselves to us as framed, but they do not extend the literary and figurative invitation that Rivers's do, to look behind them.

Rivers's work, with its boards and frames conspicuously visible, affirms its constructed character. Symbols, actors, events are represented separately, intermingled with one another, interrupted by negative space. Their combination in a single whole enables those who look at the painting to see similar operations, commonly hidden by the flow of the literary narrative, in the making of history. Certain individuals are foregrounded, others cast into obscurity or altogether forgotten. We remember P. T. Barnum; we forget John Altgeld. Certain events are similarly privileged, while others are obscured or erased. We remember San Juan Hill; we forget Haymarket. The presence of gaps and interruptions in our histories are necessary parts of their construction, yet the presentation of a seemingly uninterrupted chronology, the flow of the literary narrative, and conventional agreement on the canonical persons and events disguise the partiality of history and deny its political character.

Constructions of the future are as instructive as these diverse constructions of the past. They draw one's mind to the notion that the future is made out of the materials of the present and invite the recognition that we are consequently engaged in the constructions of the future in our quotidian activities. Because these future worlds are, like the recollections of the past, marked as constructions, they suggest the possibility of diverse futures.

Mirrors of Desire

No one who enters Tomorrowland or Epcot Center believes that they have entered the future. Few believe that the future will conform very nearly to any of the styles forecast in these constructed worlds. The recollections of other futures forecast in the past, the 1950s seen by the 1920s, the twentieth century imagined in the 1880s, are regarded as affording amusing, and occasionally informative, glimpses into the times that produced them. Our speculative constructions of future worlds are acknowledged by those who make and those who enter them as representations of our desires.

The future is thus a myth, an imagined place known to every American who ever saw the brightly colored dreams of Disneyland and Star Trek, films, comics, or "space-age" advertisements. It is all the more striking, therefore, that the future that Americans commonly conceive should be so strongly marked by features they continue to resist in the present. Americans, however conservative, however traditional, see the future as a place of equality achieved. No one sees a future of blacks subordinated to whites, of Latinos excluded, of women subordinated to men. In the future, we have often been told, women command, and starships are integrated. Racism is already understood as an anachronism. No one, whatever their present views on the social order, sees its inequalities as something to preserve. Poverty is backward. In the future everyone is not only fed but well housed, not only literate but educated. Cities are clean and bright. Industries emit no smoke and no pollutants. This is the place of our desires, shaped, as desires are, out of what we lack.

There is another future, mirroring this: the future of our fears. The cavernous cities of *Bladerunner* are the image of our fears—where the rich live in Egyptian palaces and the poor live on the streets, where corporations are more corrupt and the police more brutal, where the ads are more vivid and the people more robotic than at present. In *Terminator* and *Bladerunner,* in the made-for-TV movies of the aftermath of nuclear holocaust, the anxieties of the present have become the material conditions of an imagined future. The passage of time is marked by more repression and greater violence, by larger gulfs between rich and poor, by states and corporations that have **20** grown more knowing and more corrupt.

These architectural constructions, from period rooms in museums and presidential libraries to Williamsburg and the Old Souths and Wests of unnumbered theme parks, from *Star Wars* and *Bladerunner* to Tomorrowland, inscribe a commentary on the making of history on the American landscape. They present past and future as constructions of the present, making these rooms, these parks, monuments to their authority. In the experience, as in the construction of these pasts, Americans appropriate their history. Nevertheless, there is in this assumption of authority an oblique acknowledgment of the inaccessibility of the past. The pasts that we reconstruct are marked as pasts we make for ourselves. The future worlds we momentarily inhabit are marked as the realizations of our own desires, our own anxieties. We instruct ourselves in interpretation, in the illusions, authority, and inadequacy of representation.

Eco sees the American constructions of the past as artifacts of "a philosophy of immortality as duplication." It is not immortality but distribution that duplication aims at. America boasts innumerable copies of the Last Supper, of Michelangelo's *David,* of *La Gioconda* and the *Pietà.* Princeton and the University of Chicago have their reconstructions of (the same) Oxford Hall. Skokie, Illinois, possesses a slightly smaller (but no less arresting) reconstruction of the Leaning Tower of Pisa.

Many have deplored this cheapening of art. They claim that something is lost (I would agree that it is) in the transplantation of the *Pietà* to Forest Lawn, the appearance of Michelangelo's *David* in a Pizza Hut. Much is lost when one sees Goya's "Black Paintings" in reproduction or Angkor Wat in a photograph. These losses are not, however, the only losses that cultural critics have deplored. When an object of acknowledged beauty, a work of great cultural import, becomes known to all, it ceases to serve as a shibboleth. The man who speaks of the beauty of the Taj Mahal may be neither well traveled nor well-read; the woman who knows of Gauguin may have got her knowledge from a cereal box. One cannot fix their class. The loss of this signification of class is not something to bemoan but something to celebrate. As Eco notes however, not all of the American constructions are perfect duplications. Many offer more. Some of those he saw were moved from two to three dimensions; some were enhanced in size or color, "obviously more polished, shinier, protected against deterioration."[6] Ascribing to himself "the cultivated European" and to "the Europeanized American" a more discerning eye than he ascribes those lesser breeds "the average family, the tourist, the politician," Eco assumes that these Americans remained unconscious of the difference between their fabrications and the realities they signified. When he forgets himself in wishing that the alligators in the Mississippi appeared with the dramatic regularity of a gator in Bayou Disney, he assumes that the Americans were similarly seduced. It is not so.

21

Americans in Disneyland do not mistake it for reality. Rather, recognizing it as a representation of desire, they celebrate their collective capacity to produce a world more rational and more rewarding than that which Providence supplies them. In their play, as in their politics, they know themselves as the creators of a new world order.

Novus Ordo Seclorum

The passion to surpass the God of Nature in the making of a world manifests itself in every aspect of the life of Americans: in where they live and what they eat, in what they wear and where they play. All people, in the building of houses and the cooking of food, endeavor to give themselves better shelter and sustenance than Providence, or Nature, affords them. They not only preserve their food, they cook and season it. They not only make shelters for themselves, they line these self-constructed caves with carpets and equip them with all the conveniences a competitive imagination can contrive.

The American love for appliances and gadgetry, about which we amuse even ourselves, is not simply tinkering for tinkering's sake, the diversion of the born technician. Nor is it, as some have claimed, merely the passion for money, which prompts one to make whatever piece of foolery another will buy. It is part of the passion for a new world order. It is a challenge to God, a little playful braggadocio on the edges of a greater competition. There is no pleasure that cannot be enhanced, no pain that cannot be lessened, no effort that cannot be eased, no want that cannot be supplied, no need so small that it need not be answered, no provision so complete it cannot be improved.

Consider the kitchen. Food and shelter are not enough. It is not enough that the shelter has windows, and the food is preserved out of season. It is not enough that fire and water come at will, and predators are absent. One must have a garbage disposal, a blender, a Cuisinart, a toaster, a microwave, the things that flip and poke and stir and scrape, and the little thing that minces the garlic, a can opener, a coffee grinder, Roach Control, a waffle iron, and a cappuccino maker.

Each of these can be improved. The refrigerators can be made with ice and water in the doors; the little thing that minces the garlic can be accompanied by a rubber gadget that cleans its holes. The blender can be made with three or five or ten speeds; the insecticide can come with birth control. The words *new and improved* are emblazoned on so many wrappers at the grocery, so many boxes at the hardware store, that scarcely any American takes any notice of them. It is in these unnecessary, unwanted improvements that we display ourselves most playfully and triumphantly. The knife that cuts more quickly and surely than tooth or claw or a sharpened rock is not the end of human enterprise. There are always sharper knives, knives with handles, knives for cutting meat and cheese, a knife with a guard for opening oysters. Beyond these there is the Vegematic. The long litany of things the Vegematic did was not simply an account of the use one could make of it: it was an invocation of omnipotence. It put everything that one could need at hand. That it was so trivial a matter—the need so slight, the price so cheap—only increased the magnanimity of the offering.

Americans retain a taste for these instrumental economies. The Swiss Army knife, with its compact armory of tools; the manicure kit; the first aid kit; the pocket office with stapler, ruler, tape, magnifying glass, and folding scissors that fits in the palm of the hand; and the RV with beds and a kitchen and a color TV are attempts to make us prepared for every change in fortune, omnipotent, and independent. They are the manifestations of a Machiavellian foresight. They buy us time, extending our power within the narrow limits of our temporality. They arm us against the vicissitudes of fortune, against the hardships and indifference of the natural world.

That world too can be remade. If the experience of man in the natural world is often one of trial and scarcity, then that is evidence enough of the world's imperfection. The woods, the beach, the meadows, and the lakes can also be made new and improved. Consider the pool. The water itself is clear and (due to a certain chemical fortification) pure, without snakes or pond life or sewage overflow. It can be made (with carefully chosen plastic and paint) as blue as the Caribbean, or as dark and iridescent as a forest pool. There is no slimy mud on the bottom; there are no sharp rocks, no unexpected drops. It is long enough for swimming, deep enough for diving. There are no predators here, for the predators have been remade as well. The alligator becomes an inflatable raft, large enough to hold a man, but not equipped to eat him. The killer whale and the shark are similarly altered, made into rafts or toys or life rafts for cocktails. The creatures that threatened humanity in nature are recreated as the whimsical playthings of civilization, and a source of fear becomes a source of pleasure.

These alterations are not, of course, limited to the creatures of the deep. We give our children not only lambs and bunnies to cuddle but (perhaps more often) panthers, tigers, and bears, the velvet tyrannosaurus and the lilac pterodactyl.[7] Our children lie down with lions. They bathe with the fleet. When they are older they are taken to the zoo, where the animals, though considerably larger, rougher, and less companionable, are nevertheless in their sight and under their power, a source of pleasure. When they are grown, they may fly to the Serengeti (or to the television) to watch the animals in a more natural (but no more dangerous) setting. The predators remain, however, neither a threat to our species nor a challenge to its sovereignty.

Representation thus endeavors to transform the human experience of nature from one in which scarcity, helplessness, and fear are coupled with pleasure into an experience of unmixed pleasure and unchallenged mastery. Nature is only partly subdued. There are floods and tidal waves, fires and earthquakes. Water moccasins infest fishing holes, and bears continue to consume the occasional camper. Yet these circumstances are subordinated in the American understanding to the experience of nature as tame and beneficent, subject to our rule. The aristocratic assumption of mastery that representation engenders marks all confrontations with nature. The bear who eats one's (badly protected) provisions in the Shenandoah Valley is an amusement or an inconvenience; the bear who eats a camper in Yosemite is an aberration. Each is just one bear, after all, and not representative. The real bears, apart from us yet subject to our gaze, are seen on National Geographic specials.

Representation enables those still subject to nature to know themselves its masters. This is neither naivete nor delusion. It is representation that gives us mastery. The mastery that we acquire permits an imperfect overcoming, a partial evasion, of nature's rule of the body. We may age later and more gracefully, we can avoid or overcome certain predators and diseases, we can insure ourselves against flood, but we will feel pain, we will age, and we will die. Still, representation confers a more perfect mastery in the mind. We come to conceive ourselves as, if not the rulers of nature, natural rulers. We escape, if not nature's rule in the body, at least nature's rule in the mind, recognizing ourselves as masters in another realm. We are less eager to recognize that in willfully abandoning the natural for the symbolic order we may merely have exchanged one master for another.

The Value of the Artificial

America is a money economy, in which the media of exchange are currency and credit, written representations of worth, artificial value. Currency has moved, under the ascendancy of representation, from a representation of gold, and then silver, which might at any time be exchanged for the material it signified, to an empty signifier, supported by faith in the stability and resources of the regime that gives it currency. Virtually valueless in themselves, these bits of paper emblazoned with the likeness of other signifiers may surpass in accepted value many things whose material worth surpasses theirs. They are surpassed, in emptiness and significance, by the manipulation of credit.

Money, a signifier of value, has also come to serve, in America, as a signifier of status, a measure of one's relative success or social rank. Class, in the European sense, is deconstructed in America, fractured into traits of birth and education and a facility with social forms, which need not coexist with wealth or in a single individual. Nevertheless, income level has been privileged as a signifier of class, in popular culture as in the work of sociologists and policy analysts. It is acknowledged as the principal determinant of social class in America even by those groups who might privately privilege other traits.

Not only custom but the law instructs us that we are to take income as currency for persons. America has long recognized the legal creation of persons. The corporation has become an institution whose existence is completely taken for granted in America. It is forgotten not only that the founders of the regime once protested vociferously against its institutional establishment but also that people once found the possibility of the creation of fictive bodies, invested by the regime with rights, to be an effete fiction, an absurdity, or a fraud. Now these corporations, recognized by the regime as legal bodies, are recognized by the culture as well. They personify themselves in advertising as well as law, incarnating the companies' real or affected attributes in a material form contrived for the purpose.

Perhaps the most-telling indication of America as an economy of artificial value is the rise in number and prestige of activities concerned not with the production or the exchange of goods but with the manipulation of money or stocks—that is, with value itself. These have acquired increasing importance in the determination of the organization, activities, value, and survival of corporations in America.

The Lottery

In the lottery the triumph of the sign, of artificial value, is celebrated with the same playfulness that marks other challenges to nature and to providence. In the lottery nothing counts but the sign. There is no skill, no exercise of intellect or will, no value to any attribute of individuality. One buys, with money or with credit, a bit of paper on which something is written. The inscription has no meaning, no referents, no connotations. It may, however, be invested with many.

Players may choose to play numbers that mark, in some private fashion, their birthdays, anniversaries, or addresses. They may write some code across the random sign expressing a message that will be read only by the one that writes it. They may derive their sequences according to a system, or from a device (now sold in many stores) that gives a random sequence of the appropriate length at the touch of a button.[8] None of these affects the game.

The lottery is a game played as nearly as possible within the confines of the signifier. The ticket is an inscription without meaning, without intrinsic value, perhaps without any value at all. It is bought by artificial value, perhaps from a machine. Most tickets are worth less than nothing—less, that is, than the money one paid for them. Winning tickets confer more of the same, more money, more paper, more credit. Their value is arbitrarily ascribed.

The celebration of the signifier in the lottery mocks its inward indeterminacy. These random signs may be privately invested with meaning, in the interpretations of the players and in the selection of the winners. The selection of the winners at random foregrounds the indeterminacy of the signifier. The ticket you hold may be worth millions, hundreds, a few dollars, or nothing at all. Once the value is determined, the game is ended.

The lottery stands as the mocking, playful culmination of the ascendance of the signifier over the signified. In it the indeterminacy, the conventionality, the artfulness of money are celebrated most enthusiastically. It stands at the end of a process in which these features are realized. Gambling, with its little colored chips, its wheels and shuffled cards, still retains, in its determinate odds, elements of skill, willfulness, and individuality. Slot machines remove from this the presence of another person, putting a machine in the place of a body. They divest the player of all particularity, disarming intellect and will. Yet the sign of victory is always the same and hence invested with stable meaning. The little whirling fruits, in all their color and recognizability, lack the elegant economy of representation visible, legible, in the lottery ticket.

Abstract Art and Abstract Value

The preoccupation of abstract expressionists with surface and material, with color, form, and painterliness, produced works with significance but without meaning. This privileging of form over content commended abstract art to another consequence of abstract value, the corporation. The initial resistance of corporations to an art that presented itself as opposed to convention was readily overcome as abstract art was recognized as abstract value.[9]

Abstraction had a certain social value as well for the corporation. An abstract painting, apparently devoid of historical referents, without a religious or political content, without figures, would carry no meaning and give no offense. As long as it remained a painted surface, a play of shape, texture and light, color and geometry, in accord with the office decor, it could give no more offense than a rug. As long as it remained without visible, legible meaning, it appeared to be entirely independent of ideology.

This, of course, was hardly the case. The commonplace denigrations of abstract art are especially revealing in this regard. The notion "I could make that" or "My kid (or a blind man or a chimp) could do better" was central to the reconstruction of art as abstract value. Such views denied that the value of the painting was due to the skill or the labor of the painter or to the value of the materials. Rather they affirmed that value was conferred instead by the corporation's decision to acquire it and its ability to exchange it for other things of equal or greater value. Value was determined by the name of the artist and the judgment of experts, by the price obtained at previous sales: by the market. Each of the criteria for evaluation separated the work from the labor of the artist. Art became acknowledged as a species of currency.

False Foods

Though representation precipitates people into the symbolic order, permitting them to create literary constitutions for themselves, they nevertheless retain their corporeal constitu-

27

tions, with all the obligations these impose. The need to eat remains. This preserve of necessity is no more free from representation than the remainder of American life. Indeed it is here that the ironies of representation show themselves most conspicuously.

In America those things that are labeled *food,* particularly the notorious "cheese food," are the things most far removed from nature. In the republic of signs, *food* signifies not the sustenance that nature provides but something altogether synthetic. "Natural foods" become an indulgence and a luxury, foods of choice rather than necessity. Human needs, this language implies, can be supplied synthetically, from the most improbable materials. We can provide for, we can constitute, ourselves.

The simplest of foods become the battleground in this context over constitution. Bread and milk and cereals, basic foods on which all are dependent, are "enriched" and "fortified." The language of nutrition becomes a language of wealth and conquest. The addition of artificial value enriches these foods as it enriches the regime. Their natural merits, implicitly insufficient, are supplemented by vitamins and minerals and by the addition of ingredients from other sources. This synthesis of the natural and the artificial makes them an appropriate form of sustenance for a people similarly compounded. At the same time, it implies that providence is too parsimonious. These artful alterations of nature improve it, securing a more generous provision. Providence provides subsistence, but under our own rule we flourish.

The milk, the bread, the cereal become battlegrounds in the war for independence and self-determination. They are "fortified." In strengthening them, we establish our title. By reconstituting them we establish our authority. We nourish ourselves on substances with which we have mixed our labor. We are fed not simply on the products of nature but on our own creations. In making the resources that sustain us our own products rather than simply the produce of nature, we make ourselves our own authors. At breakfast millions of Americans commemorate, trivially and unconsciously, the establishment of authority in the act of constitution.

It is not, however, by addition alone that Americans improve their foods and amend their constitutions. They do it by subtraction as well. It is in these acts that they affirm the primacy of representation. Fortified foods, with more vitamins, more minerals, may be better foods, but the best foods for one's constitution may be those with less: less salt, less sugar, fewer calories.

The salt that is not salt and the sweet that has no sugar are edible fictions. In them representation again reveals itself as a lie. Nutrasweet is better than sugar because it is what it is not. It is not nutrition. It is not sugar. It is better than sugar because it represents sugar to the senses. Through this recourse to the symbolic order, we escape the penalties of nature. Representation, as *The Federalist Papers* argues, is the means by which we Americans rescue ourselves from the consequences of our natural appetites.

Satiric Simulacra

It is not surprising to find that a people whose foods are not foods have sports that are not sports and news that is not news. The passion for simulacra, for art, contrivance, and representation, shows itself in every aspect of American life.

Sports

Even those who, like myself, look at sports with little knowledge and less liking can see in this field layer upon layer of representation. The teams are doubly named. They represent cities and (where a city has more than one) regional and class identities within those cities. They are named for actions, animals, and attributes, for occupations and signifying garments: the Dodgers; the Tigers, Cubs, Eagles, and Dolphins; the Giants and the Athletics; the Cowboys, the Brewers, and the Pirates; and the Sox (Red and White). There are also names derived from groups already established in American myth as the holders of certain attributes (e.g., the Indians) and names derived from machines, with their attendant connotations of strength, speed, and conquest (e.g., the Jets). Some names, notably the Steelers, are multiply evocative. They are invested by

29

their partisans and detractors with certain significant traits that set one apart from another. Some come to signify particular national attributes or take on a nationally significant identity.

The players are represented, several times over, by numbers. They wear numbered uniforms, which submerge the differences signified by name and number in an identity common to the team. The numbers assign them an artificial value, which is elaborated, throughout each game and in the archives of the sport, by the compilations of statistics for each player. These statistics, altered in the course of each game, present an abstract expression of the player's value. Another expression can be found in salaries and salary negotiations, in which the player is invested with artificial value in another form.

Players are represented not only by their (vast array of) numbers but by peculiar nicknames, like "Sweetness" and "the Refrigerator." These players, Walter Payton and William Perry of the Chicago Bears, were also aptly marked by these names as consumer goods. Players who make themselves conspicuous (in the game or out of it) may find themselves in newly constructed public identities, distinct, and occasionally mythic. All sports figures will find themselves "commodified." The assignment of numbers, the assessment of statistics, the determination of salaries all represent the player as a resource to be exploited. Whether that resource is employed in the game or, as in trades, as an exchange value, it is a commodity.

Occasionally, a player will recognize and attempt to control this process of commodification. The construction of a marketable public identity then comes to resemble an act of willful self-determination. Joe Namath provides a particularly self-conscious example of this experience of reconstitution. The title of his autobiography, *I Can't Wait until Tomorrow . . . 'Cause I Get Better-Looking Every Day,* suggests the constructed and artificial character of the commodity.[10] Namath's title also suggests that the process is not one of simple self-determination. The player is dependent on convention, on the market, for the determination of his value as a commodity. Though players, and, with them, coaches and athletic associations, have become increasingly skillful marketers, the players' strike of the 1987 football season suggests that they remain largely, if uneasily, unconscious of the relation of this process of commodification to their lack of self-determination.

Not only the players, coaches, and teams but the different sports themselves serve as representations in America. Each sport—baseball, football, hockey, and the rest—acquires a particular position in the culture, associations with certain classes, attributes, and values.

The most interesting sports, however, are those that derive their interest from their falsity. Roller Derby and wrestling are what they are not. (I refer here, of course, not to the ancient sport of wrestling but to its popular televised variant.) Each of these presents itself as a sport, with team and individual events, an arena, fans, coaches, scoring, statistics, and sports announcers. Each is regarded, however, as an imposture, a simulacrum of a sport. The players are wildly theatrical and explicitly representative. One may see the Ugandan Giant confront Handsome André or Hulk Hogan wrangle with the Million Dollar Man. The outcome of the competition appears to be determined as much by narrative requirements as by the skill displayed by the competitors. Nevertheless, the competition is fierce. In Roller Derby matches it was not uncommon to see one skater grab another by the hair and hurl her out of the ring, or skate by a prone opponent several times, gathering up speed, and then leap, skates and all, onto her body. The wrestlers pound one another's head on the floor of the ring, hurl one another in and out of it, jump from the ropes onto their opponents, and (not infrequently) leap from the audience to intervene in another match. It is all very amusing and utterly incredible.

The absence of carnage in these matches reveals them as fictions. The ring, which should be slick with blood and littered with body parts, is unmarked. The victor struts around the ring, and the defeated may run from the ring or be thrown out of it, but few limp, none are carried, and all are whole. The thumping taken by the Ugandan Giant affects him as little as dynamite affects Wile E. Coyote. He emerges from the explosion decisively defeated and clearly irate but not much the worse for the experience.

This surprises no one. No one is scandalized when the rules

are violated; no one is shocked (for no one is hurt) by the violence the participants employ. In these matches, the sport reveals itself as a fiction.

Wrestling and Roller Derby seem, in their elaborate imitations of more orthodox sports, to be dependent on a borrowed legitimacy. If these had indeed assumed the legitimacy of sports with their trappings, the blatant violations of announced rules and of the code of sportsmanship, the pretended violence and the all too theatrical personae, would outrage their audience. It is quite the other way. The more theatrical the players, the more absurd their origins, their costumes, and their boasting, the more they are acclaimed. The more outrageous the violations of rules, the more unsportsmanlike the contenders, the more the audience is entertained. It is not as sports that these are enjoyed but as melodrama and satire.

The violence that prevails in wrestling matches and in Roller Derby, in cartoons and in slapstick, leaves no lasting mark upon its victims, but it is hardly inconsequential. It is violence that secures victory. Disregard for the rules may draw a reproof from the referee, and the match may (in rare cases) be declared forfeit, but violence is nevertheless reiterated as that which decides the question.

Conventional sports affirm the primacy of procedure. One cannot win in baseball or football, even boxing or hockey, by simply demolishing one's opponents. Neither the records nor the audience will recognize a victory obtained in such a fashion. One must demolish them according to the rules.

The unconventional behavior of the players in wrestling, Roller Derby, and other such pursuits makes manifest this dependence of sports on convention. The ambiguous character of these unconventional sports, at once like and unlike the sports they mimic, obliges the observer to distinguish the traits that differentiate them. They are like sports in the presence of rules, referees, announcers, and associations. They differ from sports in the unconventional names, histories, and costumes of the players, in the blatant violation of written rules and unwritten codes. The recognition that these differ from other sports entails an acknowledgment of the dependence of sports on adherence to convention.

The recognition that sports are dependent, at bottom, on

convention presents a powerful challenge to the ideology that surrounds them. The athlete, even "the natural," no longer appears as one outside politics, whose activity transcends differences of culture and ideology. Sport no longer appears as a neutral arena in which the natural hierarchy of men and nations will be revealed. It is noteworthy, then, that these unconventional, theatrical sports, with their sardonic commentary on convention, are scorned by the upper, and much of the middle, class.[11] They find favor instead with those whom convention has not favored.

In their satiric commentary these ambivalent sports do not, however, place themselves outside the semiotic network. On the contrary, their mockery of conventional sports is equally dependent on convention. It is through adherence to certain of the conventions of sports (and through the violation of others) that these simulacra establish their likeness to (and difference from) conventional sports. It is through the conspicuous use of symbolism, in the construction of the players' personae and the choreography of the matches, that these sports that are not sports draw our attention to sport as a system of signs.

News

America is a nation founded by the word. Those who mark its beginnings in the scriptural polity of the Puritans, the spoken declaration or the written constitution, concur in acknowledging the authority of the word. This consciousness of language as constitutive gives the word, written and spoken, a special place in the polity.

Among those reserved liberties to which the Constitution defers are the freedom of speech and of the press. It is through the exercise of speech and writing that Americans construct those literary selves that constitute their self-determinations in the republic of signs. It is through the manipulation of texts—the Constitution, the laws, money, stocks and bonds—that they realize themselves within the confines of their political and economic institutions. It is in the primacy of representation that republicanism and capitalism make common cause.

It is at this nexus that the news appears. The publication of the news is an activity financed by advertising and (much less importantly) by subscription. Through their subscriptions, and their purchases of single newspapers, readers exchange currency for currency: texts whose value is conventionally determined for a text whose value lies in its determination of convention. The news gives currency to events. The selection of a set of circumstances, actions, conditions, and actors, the association of these, their transformation into literary form, their publication and dissemination invest certain acts, actors, places, and events with value and diminishes the value of others. Each of these is embedded in several semiotic networks. Each becomes associated with certain others in a story. As a metonymic signifier of the story, these component parts may take on an altered significance in contexts outside the story.

A series of works by Andy Warhol offers an ironic commentary on this process of news making. In each of these works a photograph already identified as news is isolated. The isolation that once made it a news item now makes it a work of art. Through this gesture, Warhol drew attention to the artful, constructed quality of the news, and particularly to isolation as a means of conferring significance. The photographs are overlaid with color, an act suggesting, through a blunt colloquialism, that the news is similarly colored by those who present it. Whether news item or work of art, the photograph is invested with value by this process of isolation and coloring; it acquires (and serves as) currency in a system of signs. It becomes a commodity.

Warhol's series offers a commentary on news making as an art and a process of commodification. By altering the medium in which the photograph is represented, Warhol altered its significance. In doing so he drew attention to the relation of form to content in the determination of meaning. By altering the context in which the photograph was represented, he drew attention to the way in which the practices of reporting, the conventions of news making, inform the news. By making news (in every sense) at the Factory, he revealed news as a product of those factories who label their work on banner, logo, and masthead.

A different, but equally revealing, commentary can be read in the *National Enquirer,* the *Midnight Globe,* and the *Star.* In these, the medium of representation remains constant, and the content alters. These have the form of newspapers; they are printed in the same type on the same cheap newsprint. They have the same ink that comes off on your fingers, the same headlines and bylines and mastheads. They contain stories, reported by reporters, edited by editors, published by publishers, and sold at newsstands. They contain advertisements. They are commodities. They are artful. They give currency to those   **35** things that figure in their stories.

These journals are what they are not. They are newspapers in form, but with a different content. The stories they contain, with some notable exceptions, are more colorful and less credible than those of their more conventional counterparts. On a good day in the grocery line one might read about Bigfoot, women impregnated by space aliens, the Incredible Dog Food Diet, the innocent Siamese twin who died when his brother was executed by a firing squad, or the head transplants achieved by scientists. The allure of stories so astonishing, and their strategic position in the checkout lines, ensure that these newspapers are read by many. They are cited in conversation and on television, their subjects serve as metaphors, and they are long remembered, but they are not believed.

These unconventional newspapers are read by people fully conscious of their artfulness. They are reminded by the disjunction between these events and the events reported in the more conventional press, by the tone of their neighbors' voices, by the jokes on television, and by the colorful presentation of these tabloids that they are not to be believed. They are read not as fact but as fiction.

The conventional form adopted by the tabloids does not enable them to profit from the assumed veracity of the conventional press. Rather, it puts that very assumption in question. The stories in the tabloid press reveal the importance of convention in this assumption of the veracity of the press. The presentation of a story in a certain—conventional—form designates it as "fact" rather than "fiction" and instructs us to use it as such in discourse. The truth that this form imputes to it is reiterated by convention, by the agreement of subjects treated and stories appearing in other newspapers and other media.

The disjunction between the events related in the *National Enquirer* and one's own experience is rarely greater than that between one's experience and stories in the *New York Times*. One does not expect to meet Bigfoot, but then one does not expect to meet, or even catch sight of, Yasser Arafat, Mikhail Gorbachev, or the Pope. One reads a great many odd things about Michael Jackson, but then, one read a great many odd things about Nancy—and, for that matter, Ronald—Reagan. The disjunction between one's experience and what one learns from the media is not in itself sufficient to inspire incredulity. The Orson Welles radio broadcast of the *War of the Worlds* prompted a million people to flee their homes in panic at the prospect of a Martian invasion. The broadcast was cast in the form and delivered in the cadences of broadcast journalism, and it was received by some with the credence they commonly gave that form. As many have pointed out, those who listened to these broadcasts believing that they were on the edge of a *War of the Worlds* had already been persuaded that they were on the edge of a world war. They had, for the most part, little knowledge of the nations, the struggles, the ideologies, or the events related by the announcers of these news broadcasts, yet they had come to receive their pronouncements as authoritative. The announcement of another unknown enemy, another imminent and as yet invisible conflict, could draw on a reservoir of anxious credulity.[12]

Broadcast journalism, on television as well as radio, now boasts its own satiric simulacra. *Saturday Night Live* presents a news show in which fact and fiction are freely intermingled, deriving its humor in large part from the absurdity of the real revealed by this juxtaposition. Radio stations present similarly astonishing news items in a broadcast equivalent of Ripley's *Believe It or Not;* and Chuck Shepherd's "News of the Weird," a compilation of articles drawn from the mainstream, conventional press, reveals, in the words of its editors, "Weirdness, weirdness, everywhere."

The recognition that belief in the news media is, for most of us most of the time, an act of faith will instill in some a stubborn suspicion of all forms of the news media, of speeches, scholarship, and reports. They may come to take refuge in the claims of revelation; they may place their faith in theories of conspiracy. Those who have some access to sources outside the news, in books, documents, or private information, may read with these in mind, checking them against the news, the news against them. Others, lacking access to that information that would direct them either to faith or rebellion, acquiesce, quietly, faithlessly, to the conventions that indiscriminately ascribe truth to the *New York Times,* falsehood to the tabloids, moved not by belief but by the knowledge that maintenance of their social status, of their claims to rationality, depends upon acceptance of these conventions. Their concurrence is compelled not by faith in the veracity of reporters, or by a critical assessment of the evidence presented in the stories they read or hear, but by a desire to remain included in the community of discourse, the community of constructed fact, that the news media and we, in our consent to convention, create.

The recognition of the agreement between sources of news as conventional, and of one's own reliance on convention for judgments of truth and falsity, reveals the cultural significance of convention in the construction of truth. This profoundly disquieting recognition entails another, equally unsettling. The disjunction between one's experience and "current events" contains a pointed reminder of one's distance from the centers of cultural power, of one's lack of authority over the discursive networks in which one is embedded, and of one's alienation from the events and actors that constitute one's collective life. The recognition that what we commonly take for the "real" world is a convention is thus accompanied by the realization that we are commonly excluded from it.

Innovations in the presentation and content of the news suggest that those who trade in this commodity are not unconscious of the alienation that may accompany its reception. Newscasters have become more informal in their presentations, more colloquial in their speech. The news has come to include "human interest" stories, accounts of cultural trends, surveys of public opinion. In these strategies, the primacy of representation shows itself once again. Each of these strategies invites people to regard themselves as included in the news. The human interest stories suggest that they, in their singularity, may someday figure in the network news, if only for the now proverbial fifteen minutes. The polls and surveys imply that they are already newsworthy, at least in some collective capacity. Each of these strategies depends, however, on the acceptance of rep-

САNaN AN

---

resentation. One must see the figures in the human interest stories, and the figures in the polls, as in some sense surrogates for oneself.

Survey Research

38 The regard for surveys and statistical data extends very deep into American political culture. Such studies furnish stories daily to all forms of the news media; they are assessed in the deliberations of parties, candidates, agencies, and officials. For many years, they occupied a similarly privileged position in academia. Those who manipulated quantified data, and contrived varied methods for doing so, were thought to possess the only "methodology" worthy of the name.

The structure of the enterprise illuminates this privileged status, for it reveals that survey research reflects, in ironic counterpoint to its early claim to scientific neutrality, certain conspicuous cultural predispositions. In survey research as in electoral institutions, legitimacy is determined by adherence to procedure. In survey research, as in governmental institutions, representation has primacy. A choice of responses, however limited, is regarded as permitting self-expression. The practice of survey research presents itself as, ideally, endlessly replicable, as outside history and accessible to all.

Survey research is an exercise in representation. The subjects of the research are represented as individual units, "respondents," and in terms of classificatory categories ("black," "Republican," "male," "Texan"). The issues examined are isolated from the contexts in which they are commonly confronted, and presented as the subject of questions, in the context not of a dispute but of an investigation, in which the respondent participates not as a party to a debate but as a source of information and an object of study. The responses may be represented in codes. The respondents are then reconstituted into fictive communities of opinion: the 15 or 40 or 70 percent whose responses are coded alike. The results of this process of reconstitution through representation may then be represented again in words rather than numbers, in the prose conventionally used in journal articles.

These nested representations, which transubstantiate

speech to words, words to numbers, people to words and numbers, and parties to percentages, necessarily alter the things they signify. People appear in these surveys, divested of characteristics they regard as significant, marked by traits they were unconscious of or uninterested in. They are linked to people and to groups for which they have no conscious affinity and combined in associations they might vociferously reject.

Those who are surveyed have a constitution imposed upon them. Their words are not their own. In the transubstantiation of private opinion and personal expression to an already chosen, differently phrased, response, and again in the transubstantiation of that response to a number in association with others, the respondent is subject to the authority of the researcher. In supplying respondents with answers, the researcher speaks for them; they are deprived of their voices as the researcher's voice is made their own. The communities they form are not the product of their authority but the researcher's. They cannot speak to one another within them.[13]

This process, like representative government, is said to produce more legitimate results, to express the will of the people, or some portion of it, better than they express it themselves. The intervention of procedure in the act of representation is said to present collective preferences in a clearer and more accurate form, cleansed of extraneous details. The selection of responses, like the election of representatives, is constructed as an exercise in liberty, an expression of one's individual preference, interest, or will. The possibility of a choice between responses is offered as evidence of liberty and the possibility of self-expression. The procedure, however, constrains the will and limits self-expression. The respondent is confined not only in the form of the survey but in the content of the responses supplied.

The resemblance of survey research to an election, of responses to votes, has not been lost on practitioners. They have been reluctant, however, to examine the experience of confronting a choice that is not a choice, an exercise in liberty as an experience of impotence, that is commonplace among the electorate.

In order to have this experience at all, you must transform yourself from citizen to voter. This new identity is another acquired in writing. If you are to vote, you must first register. The complexities and inconveniences of this process have been much examined, and I do not rehearse them here. Through them, you use writing to obtain another written identity. You are given a voter registration card. When you arrive at the polls, you may be asked to produce the card, and you will be asked your name. If you are to be permitted to vote, your name must appear on the rolls. You will then be asked for your signature. Having been twice written and twice read, you are then permitted to write once more: to vote. The old Chicago jokes about the voting habits of the dead do more than ridicule the corruption of the "machine"; they recognize the discrepancies between the identities of citizen, resident, and voter. Representation of embodied, rights-bearing citizens in writing makes possible the introduction of simulacra on the rolls.

We are told from childhood on that voting is the exercise of a fundamental right denied to many, that it is "participation": the fullest expression of one's involvement in, and power over, the government. It is. Yet few of those who enter the voting booth and mark their ballots experience this practice as a freedom. Instead we commonly find ourselves confronted with a choice of candidates we had little or no part in selecting. Many of us see our votes as a choice for "the lesser of two evils." Few of us experience voting as an exercise of power.

Other, more trivial, aspects of the voting experience increase this sense of impotence. If you are in a politically active neighborhood, you may have to wait hours to vote. When you enter the voting booth, you are dwarfed by a large machine in a small space. The machine is plastered with warnings. You realize that you might accidently vote for the wrong person. You may not know that such mistakes can be undone. If you do, you know that such corrections will involve time and embarrassment. These features, for all their triviality, inflect the experience of voting with a pervasive anxiety. Voters are reminded by them that this is a system they do not control and whose functioning they understand only imperfectly.

The structure shared by survey research and the elections that are so often its object has profound consequences. Each is a literary undertaking, entailing the creation of fictive selves and the privileging of these above their material referents. In both cases, the opinions represented are constructed as superior in authority to opinions expressed less formally elsewhere. This claim rests, in each case, on a privileging of method, of procedure. The results of survey research, or the results of elections, may be rendered uninteresting or unimportant by the expression of conflicting opinions in another arena. Demonstrations, riots, a flurry of writings, or a change in social practice may indicate sentiments and concerns that went unrevealed in these processes of selection. These indications of discrepancies between the representations and the popular sentiment that they purport to represent do not greatly discommode the advocates of either practice, for the legitimacy of these is judged not by their content but by their form. They are not impugned by evidence that the representation does not have the value they ascribe to it. They are impugned by violations of procedure. 41

The privileging of form over content, of the procedure over what it produces, shows itself most conspicuously in the identification of quantitative social science with the term *methodology*. There are, of course, a variety of methods in the social sciences, but a course on "methodology" (or even the more elegant "methods") will rarely treat them. The student so instructed will remain ignorant of historical methods, of hermeneutics, of analytic philosophy, of semiotics, of investigative fieldwork. They will learn survey research and statistical methods. If they are fortunate, they may be introduced to certain techniques derivative of economics: rational choice and formal theory. The claim to hegemony implicit in the name *methodology*, though not without interest, may be less significant than the blunt identification of the discipline with method. This identification establishes procedural rigor as the criterion for legitimacy, and methodological sophistication as a determinant of prestige.

Here, the development of quantitative social science parallels the development of law in America. As Tocqueville observes, the emphasis on procedure in law issued, in America, in the creation of a distinct language, a body of knowledge, a set of practices and institutions, and, most importantly, an elite conversant with these. Tocqueville sees this elite as exercising a salutary restraint on the tendency of democracy to rapid and intemperate change. He sees the presence of the elite as recouping, in its adherence to order and custom, its sense of time and precedent, some of the lost virtues of aristocracy. The quantitative social sciences are, like the law, preeminently conventional. Like the law, they tend to mute change by representing it in accordance with established forms. They lack, however, the law's overt regard for history, its attention to the passage of time, and its instructively overt commitment to the preservation of privilege.

42

In survey research a singular opinion is insignificant. Opinions must be counted if they are to count at all. They must be agreed upon, and they must fit within established categories. Those opinions that are counted more often are presumed to count for more. Political influence and political efficacy are identified with numbers. The intellectual or rhetorical merit of a response becomes irrelevant in the context of the survey. The power of a particular opinion, a particular turn of phrase, to enlighten or persuade, even to incite, cannot be discerned, acknowledged, or admitted by the procedures of survey research.

The reliance on representation in survey research, like the reliance on representation recommended in *The Federalist Papers,* suggests that people cannot—or should not be permitted to—express their preferences without the intervention of a higher authority. Without the intervention of the procedures of survey research, their responses might be incoherent, too idiosyncratic to render them conscious of their common interests or preferences or perhaps too radical for the survey (or the polity) to accommodate. The intervention of the researcher casts them into communities of thought and interest, in accordance with already-established issues and positions. In doing so, the researcher becomes the author of their collective identities, in consensus and dissent.

These structural indications of suspicion of democracy stand in contradiction to presentations of the discipline as preeminently democratic and egalitarian. The method is praised for its accessibility. The construction of each individual as a unit equivalent to all others is accompanied by the construction of the discipline as open to all. As one practitioner told me and a roomful of graduate students at Princeton University, "Anyone with a high school education and a Michigan codebook can do what I do." Few disciplines would regard this as a point of pride. Survey research, however, depends for its validation on the reproducibility of its results. The statement "anyone can get these results" is not a modest one. It is a claim to truth.[14]

One may read in survey research, as in the newspapers, a cultural conflation of convention and truth. The presence of agreement—of results, among researchers, of stories, among the people—is taken for the presence of truth. Much may depend on whether or not one construes convention as the author of truth. The concurrence that it serves to signify truth is, however, sufficient to give it currency in a culture where representation has primacy.

43

The Convention of Representation

The privileging of representation in the American regime shows itself, in these literary aspects of the American constitution, as a privileging of convention. Convention is a curious, ambivalent amalgam. The word refers to an authoritative fiction. A convention is imposed. It is obeyed without reason; it usurps the will. In conventions, one is subject to the will of others. A convention is also, however, a willful and authoritative assembly acting on its own behalf or in the name and by the will of others. In these conventions, one rules the wills of others. The ambivalence that shows itself in the word *convention*, as in the acts of representation that led us to it, represents the ambivalence of the citizen who is, as Rousseau recognizes, at once subject and sovereign through convention.

Naming

The 1960s saw a curious cultural flirtation with the correspondence theory of language. There was a vogue, in fashion and decoration, in high art and popular culture, in paintings and toys, for the attachment of names to things. In fashion and in decorating, this showed itself in the labeling of any object that would take a name. The word was attached to the thing it represented, as if to reaffirm the connection, or to invest a general concept with the materiality and particularity it had lost. At the same time, the name became part of the design, investing the object with a beauty and significance it would not otherwise possess.

The fashion for giving things their names was, however, no more than a play with correspondence. Objects could be identified by their names, but they could also be given the names of others. The use of names to establish not intrinsic character but ownership was practiced with equal enthusiasm. Children had labels sewn into their clothes and taped on their lunch boxes. Adults had their names engraved on Christmas cards. The practice of labeling was taken a step beyond possession by a new instrument, the Dymo labeler. This instrument, which is still used and sold, though not with the enthusiasm that accompanied its introduction, prints out thin self-adhesive labels in white on brightly colored strips of plastic. Its most desirable and distinctive feature was not, however, color or convenience but the fact that the label could say anything one wanted. It was a means for producing little texts, or even rather long ones, that could be attached anywhere one pleased. It was an instrument of playful authority.

Names, like other texts, could be detached from their proper places and given to others. What was true of objects in this regard continued to hold true for people. The movement of one name to another is common enough in the social practice. The name of the father, and sometimes the mother, is given to the children; the name of the husband is still, sometimes, given to the wife. Throughout the postwar period, the ability to detach names has been exploited in popular culture. The representation of identity by dog tags and a social security number became commonplace in the first half of the twentieth century. The attachment of labels and numbers to people provided a very malleable metaphor.

It could convey an affectionate possession. The custom of "pinning" girlfriends was followed by the practice, common in the 1960s, of conveying affiliation, if not possession, by wearing one's boyfriend's ID bracelet. The ID bracelet itself became a common item of male, and sometimes female, dress among the young. For men, the ID bracelet recalled an earlier, more martial labeling, prominent in the mythology of World War II. The labels men wore, whether fraternity pins or ID bracelets, were identified with masculine collectivity. The practice of giv-

ing them to women provided a material means of doing what
men already did conventionally: write their names on women.
The soldier's dog tags conveyed selfless service and personal sacrifice. The convention that he reveal only "name, rank,
and serial number" to the enemy conveyed that those captured
continued to act as signs rather than themselves. They figured
not as individuals, with private lives, but as representatives and   **45**
agents of the state, with offices and public duties. In the waning
years of the Vietnam War the names of soldiers took on different connotations. Bracelets, each engraved with the name of a
soldier missing in action or a prisoner of war, were worn by
people at home in gestures of semiotic adoption. The tender-
ness toward the name would show itself later, and more completely, in the Vietnam War Memorial in Washington, where
people kiss the carved names of the dead.[15]

For the living as for the dead, names take the place of the
embodied being we have lost. In being called by name, we are,
in Althusser's term, *hailed*. We recognize ourselves in the mirror
of the name. Ideology, and the framework of practices and institutions that realize it in the material world, " 'recruits' subjects (it recruits them all), or 'transforms' the individuals into
subjects (it transforms them all) by that very precise operation
which I have called *interpellation* or hailing."[16] In "I" and
"me," in "individual" and "consumer," in "man" and
"woman," in "owner" and "viewer," we hear the "hey you!" of
the culture, and we turn around. We are, Althusser writes, "always already subjects."[17] We recognize ourselves in categories
constituted before our arrival on the scene.

In such a world, as Michel Foucault writes, perhaps our
aim must be "not to discover who we are, but to refuse who we
are."[18]

Culture of Consumption

MAN, ACCORDING TO HEGEL, to Marx, and to many who have worked less prominently in the world, realizes himself through labor. In the conception and the creation of goods, men discover and exercise the powers of their minds, their senses and their hands. They extend their knowledge, the acuity of their senses, and the dexterity of their hands. They discover, in the transactions they undertake to obtain the resources necessary for their work, in their exchanges of goods, in their reliance on the skill of others for the completion of their designs, that they are bound with other men by the conditions and the character of their being. They are dependent upon them for resources; they are like them in the coincidence of matter and ideal. They are like one another in their labor.

Each product that a man creates represents him in the world, in accordance with a system of meaning that owes less to the form or function of the act or object than it owes to historical designation. The singular works of an artist, though no less dependent on others for things necessary to their creation—paints, brushes, clay, and references—represent the creator as an individual. The products created by workers on an assembly line, though no less the product of the labor of separate men, represent them as a collectivity, working in common, and illustrate with particular clarity their dependence on one another in the creation of the product. In each case, however, it is in the thing produced and, more importantly, in the act of labor that men see themselves in the external world. They recognize themselves in representation.

I refer to the male gender here not merely because it is consistent with Hegel, Marx, and the rest nor simply because the theory speaks more directly to the experience of men than women. The activities the word *labor* designates are radically different for men and women. In one sense, and in one context that has come to color all, woman's labor does not represent her in the world but on the contrary results in the presentation of another. Domestic labor, directed at the sustenance of others, similarly effects the obliteration of the laboring woman as an individual in the social order.

Labor and Leisure

Labor is accomplished and experienced in different historical contexts, in different political and industrial institutions. The recognition of labor as an act likening all workers to one another may be experienced as the consciousness of a universal and empowering solidarity or as the obliteration of the individual self. Those who work against their will, with no power over the processes and no desire for the acts of their employment, find neither liberation nor illumination in their work. Such labor imposes a uniform impotence. Those who engage in it find themselves, collectively, diminished. Where other social institutions and spheres of action guarantee rights and offer the erstwhile laborer an experience of choice and consent denied at work, this subjection in the workplace may be regarded as entailed not in the regime but in the activity of labor. Thus the abridgement of democracy may secure, as it does in the United States, the alliance of coercive systems of production with democratic institutions. The exclusion of democracy from the workplace when it is present elsewhere marks labor as an activity where freedom is absent.

Those who have washed dishes or floors, or waited tables, or answered phones, filed, and typed, or otherwise engaged in the myriad activities of service occupations commonly experience these as areas where liberty is denied to those who work. Labor here, as in industrial production, is identified with the offices, hierarchical position, and the political infirmities of servitude. This is particularly true of domestic labor. Domestic labor in the United States has traditionally been performed by subaltern groups, especially women and African-Americans. For both, confinement within the household once marked them as the property of their master. They bore his name; they were confined within the extended body that title to property gave him in the household.

Testimony to the construction of work in the home as subjecting women can be easily and clearly read in a series of advertisements that purport to champion it. In each advertisement in *Good Housekeepings'* "New Traditionalist" campaign, the woman stands in a room with all access to the world cut off. The windows are shown closed, there are no doors, and she is confined. The text covertly reiterates this: she "looks over the fence": she is fenced in. The text on gender relations is still more striking. In one ad, the male child smiles in his mother's embrace; the female child, who appears unhappy or afraid, is not so embraced. In the second, the male child, conventionally dressed, is once again embraced. The female child, stiff in a ballet tutu and a prim cardigan, stands apart. She wears not the leotard and tights of a student dancer, the uniform of an art, but a rhinestoned costume. In the third there is no female child at all. The male child, always smiling, always embraced, carries a violin. He is already invested with property and the means to independent creativity.[1]

These advertisements articulate traditional gender relations with extraordinary clarity. Labor within the home is reaffirmed as the province of women. Boys are well served by this system, happy, cared for, and loved. Girls are neglected, and women are confined. Labor, at work or in the home, is seen as subjecting. Leisure in such a system is, by contrast, experienced as that which gives access to political power. Outside the workplace a citizen in the United States enjoys rights regarded (not within the workplace) as inalienable. Outside the workplace one may engage in political activity. Outside the workplace one may exercise choice in the selection of ends and the means to them, in the exercise of intellect and will on trivial as well as important matters.

Labor is experienced as subordination. Leisure is experienced as the realm of political and social independence. Production is experienced as constraint, consumption as the exercise of freedom and choice. Consumers exercise choice not only in the acquisition of goods but in the representation of their sentiments and themselves, for consumption is a semiotic activity. The structural bond between capitalism and democracy in American political culture lies, both ideally and materially, in the primacy of representation in the American liberal regime.

There is, however, one form of labor that is marked in American political culture as a source of freedom and a means of self-determination. This is agriculture. In recognizing the activity of providing one's own sustenance as a form of ideal as well as material, political as well as physiological, self-determination, early American agrarians (Jefferson, John Taylor, John Randolph) seized on an element of Locke that liberalism and liberal institutions neglected. They recognized that the requirements of the body—the need for food in conditions of scarcity, the dependence entailed in the acceptance of another's provision—determined the individual's political as well as physical constitution and nourished certain social institutions long after they had answered the needs of individuals. Political independence, as well as individual survival, depended on the ability to provide for oneself.[2] Agrarian radicals presented recurrent, and occasionally effective, challenges to the alliance of democracy and capitalism in American political culture. They were able to do so because they acknowledged consumption as a form of ideal and material self-determination.

The recognition of labor as subordination and constraint did not, however, inevitably issue in anxious distrust or outright condemnation of the structures and conditions of industrial or domestic labor. It did not do so because the structures of capitalism in America offered an alternative venue for the self-determination and self-expression absent in the workplace: the practice of consumption.

Commodities as Signs

Throughout American culture there are conscious and implicit recognitions that it is not merely in the production but in the consumption of representations that one leaves one's mark upon the world. It is not production (which is seen as denying individuality) but consumption (which enhances it) that is marked as the means of self-determination. Americans collectively acknowledge that these works of body and mind, these products and commodities, are invested with meaning independent of their function.[3] They continually elaborate and refine these meanings, imposing on commodities layer upon layer of reference and signification. From these products, everywhere acknowledged and employed as signs, they fashion a common language. In this language, as in the languages of their Constitution, they fashion new and various identities for themselves. The language of commodities becomes constitutional in practice.

In what they own, in how they furnish their homes, in what they drive, and most of all in what they wear, Americans endeavor to represent themselves. In doing so, they employ their products as a system of signs. Through these they represent themselves. Possessions indicate a person's class and regional, racial, and gender identity. They reveal an otherwise invisible ideology or religion, an inclination to rebellion or conservatism. They mark Americans' occupations. They may reveal where they went to school, whether or not they are married, who they love, the causes they support, the music they prefer. They will mark more subtle traits: sophistication, rusticity, sportiness, Anglophilia, divergent conceptions of femininity and masculinity, and the ineffable but ubiquitously desired cool.

Those who realize themselves through consumption rather than through labor rely on the manufacture of commodities to satisfy not only need but desire. They require choices among products not to answer the need for a slightly milder, stronger, or biodegradable detergent, a faster or a safer car, or a dress for dinner rather than for work but to answer their desire to constitute their own identities, to reveal themselves to the world.

Capitalism and Democracy

It is in the use of commodities as a system of representation that capitalism is assimilated to democracy. Commodities are chosen, purchased, employed not merely for what they do but for what they mean. It is for this reason that products proliferate, that Americans tolerate, even encourage, the profusion of products that differ in their packaging but not in their function. The elaboration of identity, the signification of particular traits, the communication of subtle contradictions in the constitution of a literary self requires a vast vocabulary. The profusion of consumer goods, of different brands of every good, expands the vocabulary of signs available to those who write themselves upon the world. It permits the inscription of evermore subtly conveyed, evermore elaborately constructed selves.

52

This recognition of the system of commodities as a system of signs, of consumption as representation, renders the commonplace Cold War critiques of the paucity of consumer goods in the Soviet Union not only intelligible but significant. Because commodities permit the realization and inscription of the self in the world, Americans could regard the absence of consumer goods, the presence of continual shortages, and restrictions on consumption in the Soviet bloc as telling indications of the absence of freedom. Citizens who lack a choice of goods are deprived not only of the product but of what the product might signify. They are not merely inconvenienced by the lack of what would satisfy a need. They are silenced by the lack of that which could express their will. For those who realize themselves in consumption, a narrowed choice of commodities is a narrowed capacity to be represented and to represent oneself. It restricts freedom of expression; it diminishes one's ability to realize oneself in the world. It deprives one of authority.

Authority through Consumption

Through commodities Americans reveal their conceptions of their identities. Out of the resources commodities provide, they manufacture identities for themselves. Commodities serve Americans as objectifications in the Hegelian sense: as material embodiments of the ideal. Commodities serve not only to express the ideal and internal but also as objects that reveal the self to itself, carrying ideas that, apprehended in the object, will be internalized. Those who choose and buy, wear them and ride in them, reveal not only what they are but what they wish to be or, more precisely, what they wish to be taken for. A male academic may present himself in class as an Oxford don, out of it as the leather-jacketed leader of the pack. A woman in law may present herself in court and the corporate office in the uniform garb of her vocation, at her friend the housewife's in a sweater with a design of beribboned Scotties that marks her wish not to be taken as a challenge. The sartorial constructions of the self, like other literary identities, enable people to be at one moment what they are not in another.

53

It would be an error to regard these constructions as lies. These seemingly deceptive self-constructions serve instead as currency for context, as indications of unvoiced intentions. Inscription endows one with the capacity to become one's own author. With this godlike capacity comes the privilege of constructing one's avatars. Through the constitution of the self in signs one can appear, after the polytheistic conception of divinity, in many forms. The woman who appears in the office as a colleague, in seminar as a threat, to her friends as bound like them in a more traditional and restrictive conception of femininity is never merely disguised, never fully revealed. As with avatars, each appearance, each constitution of the self, reveals an aspect of an identity that can comprehend many more.

In the array of self-expressions offered in commodities, "individuality" appears as merely another trait; one (like others) that can be designated through commodities. The liberal desire to express a pristine interiority, a being unlike all others, is (like all others) expressed in commodities, exploited in marketing. Individuality, one's separation from all others, is neither something we can craft nor something we can escape. It is the condition of our incarnation. Individuality, however, is an attribute that expresses itself through a well-understood array of stylistic conventions. While we profess a faith in our individuality, we treat individuality, in practice, as a style and a pose, one (but only one) of the forms in which we manifest ourselves.

The identification of the representation of the self with the acquisition of authority and the conflation of choice with consent in the employment of commodities as a system of signs, a form of speech, illustrate two principles characteristic of liberal theory. Representation through consumption merely expresses in the nominally private realm practices that govern the form of liberal institutions.

The construction of diverse representations of the self and the use of commodities as currency for context, providing public indications of what the wearer wishes to be taken for, are authoritative not only of the self but of the surrounding social context. They do more than assert the self-conception of the wearer. They assert an authority over the structures in which the author is embedded. They instruct those present that they are engaged in a particular network of meaning. By indicating the roles they are playing, the wearers offer those who interact with them an array of possible responses, and consonant roles.

The practice of consumption reveals aspects of self-determination and representative authority that liberal theory and liberal institutions have been reluctant to acknowledge. In the practices that constitute them in the world, Americans are engaged in more than self-determination. In their construction of themselves they claim more than the right to constitute the single self that liberal theory has ascribed to each. They claim instead a more liberal authority, the capacity to constitute themselves in several forms, to secure not self-determination but self-creation, the unbounded dissemination of the self. In shopping and dressing many reject the notion that they are bound to a single self. Instead they seek to construct multiple identities, to realize themselves in the world in diverse forms. In their unbounded desire for more and more they identify freedom not with fences, or with a single project of self-determination, but rather with the continual circulation of money, goods, and style and the proliferation of self-constitutions.

Consumption and Mastery

The characterization of America as a "culture of consumption" is commonly employed as a condemnation. In their insatiable desire for more products, each more trivial than the last, Americans are said to show themselves as prodigal and self-indulgent. Seduced by outward form, an extra fin on the Cadillac, a new color in bras, they show their blindness to the true significance of the products they consume with such enthusiasm. Conscious of the product only as an object, they are blind to its true meaning, deaf to the message of commonalty in labor it bears within it. In their constant desire for more and more, their readiness to buy, Americans mistake desire for need. They are seduced from desire to desire, suckered into evermore frivolous purchases.

This explanation is as much in error as the phenomenon that it describes. The Americans who buy the car with the nifty fins, or the lacey bras in pale champagne, know that these are not necessities. Consumers recognize desire as desire. In doing so, they transform consumption from an act of necessity, imposed and inevitable, into a source of pleasure and an act of will.

Subject to needs for provision, for shelter, obliged to consume if they are to subsist, they experience consumption as an imposition, need as impotence. All consumption is an act of will. In it one asserts one's power over the external world that is taken in, destroyed, digested, and made one's own. This act of will is, however, imposed by the body's constitution. In it, people are obliged to recognize that they depend upon others not merely for provision but for their constitution.

When they consume beyond their needs, in response to desires of their own making, they escape this impotence, and they acquire power. Consumption is experienced as the exercise of a will independent of the body's requirements. In it the will shows itself educated by need, but no longer in its service. Through it, Americans constitute identities of their own making, conceived in the proliferation of desires, manifest in consumption.

This exercise of self-determination, which accords so well with liberal ideology, the institutions of representative government, and the structures and the interests of capital and commerce, is not—though it is universally encouraged and universally practiced—universally applauded. The phrase "a culture of consumption" is commonly intended as a term of disapprobation. "Conspicuous consumption" is regarded as a form of arrogance or, more often, of bad taste. This ambivalence finds its fullest expression in attitudes toward groups that are themselves ambivalent.

Peripheral Consumers

The capacity to constitute oneself through consumption is, ironically, most conspicuous among those who have often had the least to spend, groups on the periphery of American culture. These groups have often been portrayed as prone to extrava-

56 gance in dress and ornament, full of desires, easily lured by the pretty and the prestigious, seduced by advertising, and given to consumption and display. The Indians, betrayed by their desires, sold Manhattan for a handful of blue beads, traded furs for firewater, and, in an excess of consumption, drank themselves into collective impotence. Women squander the provision of a benevolent patriarchy on furs and perfume and expensive haircuts. They chatter on the phone and run up enormous bills. They are "born to shop," slaves to every fashion, and their checkbooks never balance. Blacks are snappy dressers, turned out with an unseemly attention to fashion and a love of display, spending money on music and dancing, neighborhood parties and elaborate funerals, never saving. The expensively attired homosexual, the Chicano in the shiny low-rider, the immigrant with the enormous color TV are stock figures in American culture.

Though these portrayals are always overdrawn and often malevolent, though they have done much harm, I do not dispute them. I suspect that there is something true in them. I suspect, moreover, that this passion for consumption, which has been taken as a sign of economic naivete, is instead a sign of semiotic sophistication.

These groups and others on the periphery are commonly excluded, by law, custom, or the lack of resources, from full participation in American economic structures. African-Americans and women were, for many years, unable to own property in their own names, restricted from the practice of many professions, and largely excluded from manufacturing. Their confinement in service occupations, domestic labor, and agriculture restricted their participation in productive activities. Those in which they were permitted to engage—domestic labor and agriculture—were culturally constructed as activities of the body in the natural world rather than activities of the intellect and offered few satisfactions as methods of realizing oneself in the external political world. Consumption thus became, for these groups, not merely a way but the principal, often the only, way in which they could represent themselves in the world or interject themselves into public discourse.

Yet the meaning of consumption for each of these groups is not the same. Differently situated in the political structures, endowed by the culture with disparate identities and traits, they give diverse meanings to the common practice in which they engage.

57

Women

The construction of women as rampant consumers is common throughout the culture. Women are "born to shop"; they run off to shops like Wilma Flintstone and Betty Rubble, brandishing credit cards and yelling "Charge!" When they are unhappy, they "buy a new hat" or a box of chocolates. They are consoled by consumption. For a man who has offended a woman, the best way to placate her, as *Saturday Night Live* once argued, is to "buy her a nice present."

This passion for consumption, ascribed to all women, is more evident in the activities of some of their number. The shoes of Imelda Marcos have become a metonym for this excess. The racks of clothes, of handbags, the drawers of black bras, but most of all the shoes that were exhibited, row upon row, to the people who occupied the Malacanang Palace after the revolution bore witness to the rapacity of the tyrant's wife.[4] All women are born to shop, the spectacle implies. Those who find themselves with greater resources still find occasion to exceed their means. The construction of women as born to shop is one of a series of myths that presents women as voracious consumers. These myths take many forms. They present women as sexually insatiable, exhausting men, and, when they have finished with men, going on without distinction to women, or like Catherine the Great to horses. They must be confined within harems, purdah, and chastity belts or kept within bounds by circumcision. They cannot contain themselves; they must be contained.

Yet, though they cannot contain themselves, women are identified with the capacity to contain, confine, and restrict men. The capacity of women to contain, to comprehend, recalls that first containment in the mother that is common to all. There is a sense, for all of us, in which the mother has the ability to encompass the world.[5] This capacity, which recalls an early undifferentiated community, an unthought communion, a limitless state of satisfaction, also calls up fears of confinement, of the loss of oneself in the surrounding other. These fears show themselves in the ascription to women of jealousy and possessiveness, to mothers of a smothering and inescapable dominion. The womb becomes a place of confinement for men, of permanent dependence and inferiority. The vagina is a mouth, "lips that never did speak," that takes men in, reducing them again to children, or a mouth with teeth, a vagina dentata, that emasculates them. In all these constructions, the fear of consumption is inscribed on women.

Imelda Marcos belongs in a series of women whose mythic excesses of consumption have been elaborately chronicled. She was followed in the international press by Michele Duvalier and preceded by the woman who was, perhaps, the mythic referent for all: Marie Antoinette. Much can be read in this reiterated metaphor. Each of these women occupied the precincts of power. Each was constructed, in her time and after, as the "power behind the throne," whose selfish desires and insatiable appetites invited revolution. Louis XVI and Jean-Claude Duvalier figure in these myths as indolent fools, too weak to control (and too stupid to see the danger in) their wives' excesses. The incapacity of Ferdinand Marcos is ascribed not to native stupidity but to the weakness and decaying faculties that come with age and illness. In these portrayals, as in the broader and more vivid myths of the vagina dentata and the imprisoning mother, feminine consumption is marked as a threat to masculine power. The power of women to consume emasculates men; it brings down regimes. It contains a threat to structure and authority.

Feminine consumption, in these constructions, threatens not only the possession of power by men but the ascendancy of traits and faculties that culture marks, and values, as masculine. The woman who writes check after check on an overdrawn account, who makes charges she has not the means to pay, and the women who, careless of the cost, fill palaces with shoes and diamond necklaces share not only common appetites

58

but a common irrationality. They are, despite the imputation of intrigue, denied the capacity for rational calculation. They are marked as outside the money economy, indifferent to the power of the word, constantly engaged in obtaining material goods. They are shown as indifferent to money, failing to recognize the value of the word, of contract, of abstract value, constantly engaged in obtaining not more money (an enterprise that would mark them as rational and place them within the established structures of politics and economics) but more things. Their passion to exchange money for things, to obtain material goods, denies the value of money. They do not know the value of a dollar.

Perhaps they know it too well. The acceptance of money as currency, as value, is an acceptance of contract, an act of faith in regimes and, more importantly, in signification. Those who cling to money, who amass credit, who manipulate finances, express their faith in the sign. Those who cannot hold on to their money, who rapidly exchange these small pieces of coin and paper and plastic for more material goods, distrust the sign, deny that faith. They are heretics, and they raise questions that might prove embarrassing to the partisans of existing economic structures.

The profusion of shoes exhibited in ridiculous row upon row illustrated the absurdity of an appetite that extended not only beyond need but beyond desire. Surely, she did not need so many shoes. The virtue of capitalism, indeed, of civilization altogether was, however, to enable us to live beyond our needs. What was striking about the excesses of Imelda Marcos was that they seemed to challenge not only the limits of need but the limits of desire. When one had three hundred pairs of shoes could one desire another pair? Could one, indeed, remember what one had, what one lacked? What pleasure could be taken in the acquisition of the sixty-third pair of low-heeled black pumps, or even an unparalleled pair with fuchsia lizard straps? The pleasure of a pair of shoes, intense enough to those who take pleasure in the feel of leather or fine work or the play of the color of the shoes with the color of a dress, must grow less intense with every purchase. And, if that were so, how much more irrational it would seem to accumulate not only pairs of shoes (each of which, after all, she might have worn once or twice in the course of a long life) but money in the billions, which one would never spend. The translation of money into goods reveals with a sharp and subversive force the inequities in the accumulation of capital and the distribution of resources. The absurdity of the accumulation of money beyond need, beyond use, beyond all but the most abstract desire is revealed in the translation of a much more modest excess into material form.

Feminine consumption, as a metaphor for the original containment of men in the bodies of women, calls up apprehensions of feminine dominion. It also recalls a type of legitimate domination, in which authority rested not in the office but in the body. The image of the containing mother is replicated by the monarchs and aristocrats who claimed similarly comprehensive identities. The feminine capacity for consumption recalls the power exercised by an aristocracy that claimed to hold power by birth and blood in the body. Condemnations of the excesses of Imelda Marcos, Michele Duvalier, and the "welfare queens" are enhanced by their implicit recollection of the material authority of a now illegitimate, but by no means forgotten, aristocracy of the body.

The possibility of rule through the body is presented, differently, playfully, by Madonna. The femininity of her body, once an obstacle, becomes the means to wealth; her sexuality, once the means to feminine subjection, is refigured as a form of feminine power. Madonna's foregrounding of the body is not limited to her own. The bodies of gay men and women, of blacks and Latinos, figure in Madonna's work as objects of admiration. Gay blacks and Latinos appear in her work (and in her) as the creators and practitioners of a new style—as authoritative. Her construction of herself as a "material girl" subverts the hierarchies and practices evoked by its dense tissue of references.[6]

In all of these readings, materiality and the power of women are associated. Feminine power is associated with a threat not only to particular husbands but to patriarchy, not only to men but to those qualities the culture marks as male: rationality, abstraction, structured regimes, and established governments. The role of commodities in the construction and representation of identity ensures that feminine consumption will be seen as potentially, perhaps intrinsically, subversive. If money is power, the use of money is an exercise of power. Where it is turned away from itself, out from the ideal to the material, it presents a challenge not only to the structure of economic relations but to the primacy of representation.

If commodities present forms in which one can realize oneself in the world, a system of signs in which one can speak publicly, then the spectacle of feminine consumption speaks of a desire for public speech and constitutional self-expression that cannot be satisfied. The satisfaction of this desire threatens more than the entry of women into public discourse, the transfer of the power to constitute feminine identity from men to women. It threatens the prevailing understanding of the act of constitution. The woman who dresses (as women do) regally one day, democratically the next; flirtatiously, then ascetically; dramatically, then professionally, constitutes her identity not in constancy but in change. She is constantly engaged not only in the construction but in the attendant deconstruction of her identity.

Though the practice of creating multiple selves is common to men and women, it is identified as feminine and given more cultural encouragement in women. Their capacity to alter themselves is presented culturally as an aspect of feminine duplicity, and a hazard. While men are likewise engaged in this activity, it is neither acknowledged nor considered threatening—unless they are understood to be something more—or something other—than men. Male transvestites are, of course, a notable exception to this. They are noteworthy, in this context, for their semiotic, as well as their sartorial, proximity to women and for their position in the radical wing of gay political activity. African-American men, whose difference is inscribed as race, are ascribed something of the same preoccupation with style and the same deceptive relation to property.

Women and African-Americans have been constituted in the discourse of politics, popular culture, and the academy as if they were discrete groups whose interests are distinct and often opposed. The practices of popular culture, and the texts written quietly in the image, inform us, however, that we are bound together. The images of the welfare queen, prostitute and pimp, Michele Duvalier and Imelda Marcos bind race and gender in the image of a common transgression. The practices of African-Americans and women reveal other bonds, even on the single plane of consumption. African-Americans and women are (by reason of their structural position) particularly conscious of commodities as a system of signs. They employ this language as a mode of self-expression, a deconstructive commentary on identities. They value practices and aesthetics that encourage consumption: shared provision, celebrations and parties, and style. These should be read not as aberrations but as present and authoritative in American culture. Plainness, and the absence of festivity and hospitality, ought not to be elevated to the status of a standard.

African-Americans

There is layer upon layer of a poignant and dangerous irony in the images of consumption by African-Americans. One sees people owning who were once owned themselves. Relations of trade retain, when they refer to African-Americans, an association with historic exploitation. The recollection of a history of slavery—of people held as property—throws the legitimacy of all property relations into question.

The connection between consumption and the overcoming of slavery has been made explicitly by black figures in popular culture. Mr. T, in his commentaries on his rather eccentric and extravagant dress, identified his profusion of gold chains with the experience of slavery, transformed in the rise of blacks to fame and wealth. Rap groups have made the same connection. Some, however, have questioned whether or not the legacy of slavery has been overcome in the mastery of consumption, "whether black people can affirm identity by way of a brand name." Susan Willis cites Michael Jordan, who "*is* Air Nike. He is not just shown wearing the shoes like some other champion. . . . Rather, his name and the brand form a single unified logo-refrain." In Willis's view, this instance does not reflect blacks' ability to constitute themselves or speak through commodities, "rather it speaks for the commodification of Jordan himself."[7] Property relations, Willis recognizes, are not neutral nor are they the same for all who enter into them. They are imbedded in a historical context that inscribes different meanings onto different holders of property. Willis's reading of that difference is, I think, less helpful than her careful and perceptive observation of the need for it. She contrasts Michael Jackson's trickery with the commodity form with Alice Walker's refusal of commodity fetishism and attendant imagining of an organization of production. The identification of black men and white women with commodity fetishism, of white men and black women with production, reflects traditional, and misleading, conceptions of the articulation of race and gender.   **63**

Though no African-Americans have been held as property for over a hundred years, though long before emancipation free blacks held property in their own names, the relations of blacks to property continue to be problematic. Their ownership of property is often unjustly construed as suspect. The illicit conversion of African-Americans into property is echoed and inverted in the contemporary construction of a black underclass. This class, or anticlass, recalls the condition of slavery; its members are without paying jobs, without training, without social bonds. They are given over to crime. Yet they are said to be not the objects but the agents of an illicit trade.

The crimes particularly attributed to members of this class are worth noting. They are identified with theft, especially with theft to support a drug habit.[8] The identification of African-Americans with illicit consumption is writ large here. The theft, itself an act of illicit consumption, is undertaken to permit another. This pattern shows itself again in charges that recipients of public aid or private charity will defraud the givers by spending the money on drink or drugs, and in that stock figure of conservative demagoguery, the welfare queen.

This figure, carrying apprehensions of both African-Americans and women, is cited over and over again as the enemy not just of the regime but of economic justice altogether. The title *queen,* with its ironic recollection of Marie Antoinette, marks this figure as a usurper of legitimate power, as one who loots a patrimony not her own. Thus criticisms of "the welfare queen," presenting themselves as efforts to secure justice, assert through this metaphor the propriety of exclusions of African-Americans and women from the nation and economic structures.

Another, but more complex, critique of African-American and feminine consumption appears in the figure of the black pimp. Here illicit consumption is both enjoyed and offered. The pimp profits from the illicit consumption of others. The figure of the prostitute similarly reiterates the association of women with illicit consumption. She, too, offers and enjoys illicit consumption. She consumes both the body and the wealth of her patrons. She is both the illicit consumer and the illicit consumed.

64

Haitian immigrants to the United States have been given a similarly ambivalent construction as illicit consumers and illicitly consumed. Their decision to immigrate is condemned as a mere manifestation of greed, of the desire to consume, and they are carefully differentiated from Cubans, who are identified as political immigrants. Haitians are identified as a population particularly at risk for AIDS, a disease that appears to consume its victims and that is culturally constructed as the consequence of acts of illicit consumption, either of drugs or sex.

The construction of African-Americans as illicit consumers is a profound and perverse denial of a history in which they were illicitly consumed. Yet like all such denials, it carries within itself the recollection of that which it attempts to erase.

The Good Immigrant

The apprehensions that attach to consumption by women and African-Americans are not attached to portrayals of excessive consumption among recent immigrants. The newly arrived immigrant from Eastern Europe or the former Soviet Union who arrives in America with an enthusiasm for its liberal array of goods is pictured far more sympathetically. Television and movies may poke a little fun at the Croatian janitor with his lavish new color TV or those "wild and crazy guys" ready to enjoy the pleasures of American nightlife, but they do not visit on them the opprobrium given to others. Consumption by immigrants is not the same as consumption by African-Americans and women. The meaning of the act is altered by the differences in position—by differences in context and thus in meaning—among these groups.

Immigration is seen by Americans as the exercise of choice. Those who deny the right of emigration deny their people choice and the right of self-determination. Those who emigrate exercise that right of choice. Those who immigrate to the

United States have chosen America. They are Americans by choice.

Consumption, too, is an exercise of choice. Consumption by immigrants recalls their choice of new land, a new life. Their enthusiasm for American goods is read as enthusiasm for good America, the land of plenty. Their efforts to obtain all that America has to offer materially are read as signs of their efforts to obtain its ideal offerings. In America, they (and we) are told, you can have it all. **65**

Consumption among immigrants appears in this context as a constitutional act, an exercise of the right of self-determination. Their love of shops and shopping, of the restaurants and the nightclubs and the discos, is read as an enthusiasm for that capacity for choice that enabled them to become Americans. In choosing American commodities they recall their choice of the American regime. The profusion of commodities represents continued access to choice, to self-expression, to self-determination. At the same time, the immigrants' passion for American goods ensures the outcome of their choice. They will construct American identities for themselves. The desire for American goods is both a means and a metaphor for assimilation. American ratification of the exercise of choice by immigrants can be given without apprehension, for immigrant choice presents no threat.

Shopping Center and Periphery

The construction of women, African-Americans, and immigrants as consumers, and the varied meanings ascribed to their consumption, depend upon the recognition of consumption as a means of self-realization and self-expression in the American regime. Commodities, in this semiotic network, provide a vocabulary for self-expression, the materials for constituting oneself. They are the means and matter of self-determination.

Consumption, however, presents a mode of discourse in which the liminal are not only permitted, but obliged, to participate. They are confronted, however slender their means, with choices among commodities. Consumption offers a mode of discourse, and an immanent symbolic lexicon, to those who lack access to the press, to publishing, to those political and economic institutions in which some speak and write authoritatively. It offers a means of self-realization in the material world to those whose productive activity is constrained and devalued. Their manipulations of consumer goods—the clothing they wear, the cars they alter, drive, and race, the objects they put in their houses and yards—are seen by their wealthier and more powerful compatriots. They provide the means for public statements, for the inscription of texts on the external world.

Consumption also permits those on the periphery to appropriate—however partially, however nominally—the goods of the center. Consumption is experienced in childhood as a successful effort to comprehend and overcome a hostile or indifferent world, an assertion of power over the other. This understanding of consumption is constantly reaffirmed in American culture. The dogma that the market, which rules all, is itself ruled by the law of supply and demand also constructs consumption as a constitutional activity. Consciousness of this renders consumption an exercise in economic power—one of the few available to those whose access to economic structures is severely constrained.

This is not to say, of course, that consumption is experienced solely as a source of power by those on the periphery. On the contrary, they are peculiarly situated to see consumption as a relation of power with multiple dimensions. For those whose means are slight, choices among commodities become decisions fraught with anxiety, with consequences, with significance. They are constantly reminded, at the checkout counter, at the bus stop, by their bills, of their limited purchasing (and political) power. They experience the representative structures of the economy—money, credit, interest—as confining fictions. They are obliged by their condition to recognize that money and credit have significance beyond their utility for the purchase of goods. They are obliged to recognize that commodities have significance beyond their ostensible function. They are thus able to see the economy as a system of meaning, a series of semiotic structures in which one acquires power, experiences domination, establishes status, and experiences inferiority. They recognize both the force and the inadequacy of choice as an indication of consent. They recognize that the use of commodities as a system of public and political representation is at once an expression and a subversion of representative government. This necessarily enhanced sensitivity to the significance of economic relations enables those on the periphery to consciously engage in the manipulation of this system of signs, and in the constitution of an identity through it. Yet as they do so, they increasingly experience their limited purchasing power as a limitation on their capacity for self-determination. The more significant their purchases, the more they are burdened by the necessity of choosing between commodities.

    This arrangement is multiply ironic. Consciousness and the attendant capacity for semiotic action appear as the consequence of confinement and the constraints on material manipulation. As Theodor Adorno and other members of the Frankfurt School observed, the attempts of the peripheral to acquire power through the acquisition of the consumer goods that serve as signifiers of power merely increase the periphery's economic and intellectual indebtedness to the center.

    The characterization of these peripheral consumers as merely the deluded victims of capitalism fails, however, to capture the finer points of the irony. The sophisticated, initially subversive appropriations of the commodities of the center in the texts of the periphery set fashion and establish other semiotic networks. These acts of authority on the periphery penetrate and constitute meaning and identity within the center. In this moment of authority, the periphery loses control of its texts, its semiotic products. They are appropriated by the center. Though these authors on the periphery may reap the benefits of their constitution of a language in an enhanced symbolic status, a certain cultural prestige, they will rarely be able to translate these into other forms of artificial value. Instead, they find themselves recapitulating on the plane of culture the experience of exploitation in the production of material goods. They produce, the center markets, and they buy back their productions at a higher rate.[9]

    The peripheral construction of semiotic networks from the material of mass-marketed commodities apprises the center of the possibility of using significant commodities as a means for governing the construction of identity. They are able through advertising, among other means, to influence, if not control, the significance of particular commodities. The efforts of the peripheral consumer to construct a semiotic network, and an expression of identity, with these materials are increasingly frustrated by the meanings invested in commodities by those who control their production. To my mind, the most satisfying expression of the resulting panic can be found in a song by the Clash:

> I'm all lost in the supermarket.
> I can no longer shop happily.
> I came in here for that special offer
> Guaranteed Personality.

Thomas Dumm vividly evokes the anxieties of excess in his essay "Lost in the Supermarket." "I had to choose. I could not. I was expected home and I stood there, time passing." Choice becomes not an experience of freedom but of compulsion. The array of commodities replaces necessity with choice, need with desire, and in doing so imposes a need less easily satisfied, the need to choose. "A regime of choice is a regime which is every bit as forceful as that which it replaces, and more difficult to transform into something else." [10]

The purchase of commodities is an exercise of subjectivity and an act of agency, yet as Dumm observes, subjectivity and agency also disappear in choice. Commodities cast the ideal, the immanent, and the imagined into material form. They make aspects of the self real, present and tangible, yet the sense of self may disappear in the confrontation with a vast array of commodities, presenting diverse qualities, speaking to different aspects of the self. The panic Dumm describes, in the supermarket, in the store, follows from the inarticulate recognition that the available semiotic material—at once insufficient and excessive—limits the possibilities for self-determination.

Shopping at the Mall

The mall has been the subject of innumerable debates. Created out of the modernist impulse for planning and the centralization of public activity, the mall has become the distinguishing sign of suburban decentralization, springing up in unplanned profusion. Intended to restore something of the lost unity of city life to the suburbs, the mall has come to export styles and strategies to stores at the urban center. Deplored by modernists, it is regarded with affection only by their postmodern foes. Ruled more by their content than by their creators' avowed intent, the once sleek futurist shells have taken on a certain aura of postmodern playfulness and popular glitz.

The mall is a favorite subject for the laments of cultural conservatives and others critical of the culture of consumption. It is indisputably the cultural locus of commodity fetishism. It has been noticed, however, by others of a less condemnatory disposition that the mall has something of the mercado, or the agora, about it. It is both a place of meeting for the young and one of the rare places where young and old go together. People of different races and classes, different occupations, different levels of education meet there. As M. Pressdee and John Fiske note, however, though the mall appears to be a public place, it is not. Neither freedom of speech nor freedom of assembly is permitted there. Those who own and manage malls restrict what comes within their confines. Controversial displays, by stores or customers or the plethora of organizations and agencies that present themselves in the open spaces of the mall, are not permitted. These seemingly public spaces conceal a pervasive private authority.

The mall exercises its thorough and discreet authority not only in the regulation of behavior but in the constitution of our visible, inaudible, public discourse. It is the source of those commodities through which we speak of our identities, our opinions, our desires. It is a focus for the discussion of style among peripheral consumers. Adolescents, particularly female adolescents, are inclined to spend a good deal of time at the mall. They spend, indeed, more time than money. They acquire not simple commodities (they may come home with many, few, or none) but a well-developed sense of the significance of those commodities. In prowling the mall they embed themselves in a lexicon of American culture. They find themselves walking through a dictionary. Stores hang a variety of identities on their racks and mannequins. Their window displays provide elaborate scenarios conveying not only what the garment is but what the garment means.

A display in the window of Polo provides an embarrassment of semiotic riches. Everyone, from the architecture critic at the New York Times to kids in the hall of a Montana high school, knows what *Ralph Lauren* means. The polo mallet and the saddle, horses and dogs, the broad lawns of Newport, Kennebunkport, old photographs in silver frames, the evocation of age, of ancestry and Anglophilia, of indolence and the Ivy League evoke the upper class. Indian blankets and buffalo plaids, cowboy hats and Western saddles, evoke a past distinct from England but nevertheless determinedly Anglo. The supposedly arcane and suspect arts of deconstruction are deployed easily, effortlessly, by the readers of these cultural texts.

Walking from one window to another, observing one another, shoppers, especially the astute and observant adolescents, acquire a facility with the language of commodities. They learn not only words but a grammar. Shop windows employ elements of sarcasm and irony, strategies of inversion and allusion. They provide models of elegant, economical, florid, and prosaic expression. They teach composition.

The practice of shopping is, however, more than instructive. It has long been the occasion for women to escape the confines of their homes and enjoy the companionship of other women. The construction of woman's role as one of provision for the needs of the family legitimated her exit. It provided an occasion for women to spend long stretches of time in the company of their friends, without the presence of their husbands. They could exchange information and reflections, ask advice, and receive support. As their daughters grew, they would be brought increasingly within this circle, included in shopping trips and lunches with their mothers. These would form, reproduce, and restructure communities of taste.

The construction of identity and the enjoyment of friendship outside the presence of men was thus effected through a practice that constructed women as consumers and subjected them to the conventions of the marketplace. Insofar as they were dependent on their husbands for money, they were dependent on their husbands for the means to the construction of their identities. They could not represent themselves through commodities without the funds men provided, nor could they, without money, participate in the community of women that was realized in "going shopping." Their identities were made contingent not only on the possession of property but on the recognition of dependence.

70

Insofar as shopping obliges dependent women to recognize their dependence, it also opens up the possibility of subversion.[11] The housewife who shops for pleasure takes time away from her husband, her family, and her house and claims it for herself. Constantly taught that social order and her private happiness depend on intercourse between men and women, she chooses the company of women instead. She engages with women in an activity marked as feminine, and she enjoys it. When she spends money, she exercises an authority over property that law and custom may deny her. If she has no resources independent of her husband, this may be the only authority over property she is able to exercise. When she buys things her husband does not approve—or does not know—of she further subverts an order that leaves control over property in her husband's hands.[12]

71

Her choice of feminine company and a feminine pursuit may involve additional subversions. As Fiske and Pressdee recognize, shopping without buying and shopping for bargains have a subversive quality. This is revealed, in a form that gives it additional significance, when a saleswoman leans forward and tells a shopper, "Don't buy that today, it will be on sale on Thursday." Here solidarity of gender (and often of class) overcome, however partially and briefly, the imperatives of the economic order.

Shoppers who look, as most shoppers do, for bargains, and salespeople who warn shoppers of impending sales, see choices between commodities as something other than the evidence and the exercise of freedom. They see covert direction and exploitation; they see the withholding of information and the manipulation of knowledge. They recognize that they are on enemy terrain and that their shopping can be, in Michel de Certeau's term, a "guerrilla raid." This recognition in practice of the presence of coercion in choice challenges the liberal conflation of choice and consent.

Shopping at Home

Shopping is an activity that has overcome its geographic limits. One need no longer go to the store to shop. Direct mail catalogues, with their twenty-four-hour phone numbers for ordering, permit people to shop where and when they please. An activity that once obliged one to go out into the public sphere, with its diverse array of semiotic messages, can now be done at home. An activity that once obliged one to be in company, if not in conversation, with one's compatriots can now be conducted in solitude.

The activity of catalogue shopping, and the pursuit of individuality, are not, however, wholly solitary. The catalogues invest their commodities with vivid historical and social references. The J. Peterman catalogue, for example, constructs the reader as a man of rugged outdoor interests, taste, and money.[13] He wears "The Owner's Hat" or "Hemingway's Cap," a leather flight jacket or the classic "Horseman's Duster," and various other garments identified with the military, athletes, and European imperialism. The copy for "The Owner's Hat" naturalizes class distinctions and, covertly, racism:

72

> Some of us work on the plantation.
> Some of us own the plantation.
> Facts are facts.
> This hat is for those who own the plantation.[14]

Gender roles are strictly delineated. The copy for a skirt captioned "Women's Legs" provides a striking instance of the construction of the gaze as male, of women as the object of the gaze:

> just when you think you see something, a shape you think you recognize, it's gone and then it begins to return and then it's gone and of course you can't take your eyes off it.
>
> Yes, the long slow motion of women's legs. Whatever happened to those things at carnivals that blew air up into girl's skirts and you could spend hours watching.[15]

"You," of course, are male. There is also the lace blouse captioned "Mystery": "lace says yes at the same time it says no."[16] Finally, there are notes of imperialist nostalgia: the Sheapherd's Hotel (Cairo) bathrobe and white pants for "the bush" and "the humid hell-holes of Bombay and Calcutta."[17]

> It may no longer be unforgivable to say that the British left a few good things behind in India and in Kenya, Singapore, Borneo, etc., not the least of which was their Englishness.[18]

As Paul Smith observes, in his reading of their catalogues, the *Banana Republic* has also made capital out of imperial nostalgia.[19]

The communities catalogues create are reinforced by shared mailing lists. The constructed identities are reified and elaborated in an array of semiotically related catalogues. One who orders a spade or a packet of seeds will be constructed as a gardener and receive a deluge of catalogues from plant and garden companies. The companies themselves may expand their commodities to appeal to different manifestations of the identities they respond to and construct. Smith and Hawken, a company that sells gardening supplies with an emphasis on aesthetics and environmental concern, puts out a catalogue in which a group of people diverse in age and in their ethnicity wear the marketed clothes while gardening, painting, or throwing pots. Williams-Sonoma presents its catalogue not as a catalogue of things for cooking but as "A Catalog for Cooks." The catalogue speaks not to need but to the construction of identity.

The Nature Company dedicates its spring 1990 catalogue "to trees," endorses Earth Day, and continues to link itself to *The Nature Conservancy* through posters and a program in which you buy a tree for a forest restoration project. Here, a not-for-profit agency is itself commodified, adding to the value of the commodities offered in the catalogue.[20] In this catalogue, consumption is not merely a means for the construction and representation of the self, it is also a means for political action. Several commodities are offered as "A Few Things You Can Do" to save the earth: a string shopping bag, a solar battery recharger, a home newspaper recycler. Socially conscious shopping is a liberal practice in every sense. It construes shopping as a form of election, in which one votes for good commodities or refuses one's vote to candidates whose practices are ethically suspect. In this respect, it reveals its adherence to the same ideological presuppositions that structure television's Home Shopping Network and other cable television sales shows.

Both politically informed purchasing and television sales conflate the free market and the electoral process. Dollars are identified with votes, purchases with endorsements. Both offer those who engage in them the possibility to "talk back" to manufacturers. In television sales shows this ability to talk back

73

is both more thoroughly elaborated and more thoroughly exploited. Like the "elections" on MTV that invite viewers to vote for their favorite video by calling a number on their telephones, they permit those who watch to respond, to speak, and to be heard by the television. Their votes, of course, cost money. On MTV, as in the stores, you can buy as much speech as you can afford. On the Home Shopping Network, the purchase of speech becomes complicated by multiple layers and inversions.

Each commodity is introduced. It is invested by the announcer with a number of desirable qualities. The value of these descriptions of the commodities is enhanced by the construction of the announcer as a mediator not only between the commodity and the consumer but between the salespeople and the consumer. The announcer is not, the format suggests, a salesperson (though of course the announcer is). He or she is an announcer, describing goods that others have offered for sale. Television claims to distinguish itself by making objects visible to the eyes, but it is largely through the ears that these commodities are constructed. The consumer, in purchasing the commodity, purchases the commodity, what the commodity signifies, and, as we say, "buys the salesperson's line." The consumer may also acquire the ability to speak on television. Each purchase is recorded and figures as a vote in a rough plebiscite, confirming the desirability of the object. Although the purchase figures are announced as if they were confirming votes, it is, of course, impossible to register one's rejection of the commodity. Certain consumers get a little more (or rather less) for their money. They are invited to explain the virtues of the commodity—and their purchase—to the announcer and the audience. The process of production, of both the consumers and that which they consume, continues in this apology for consumption.

The semiotic identification of consumption as an American activity, indeed, a patriotic one, is made with crude enthusiasm on the Home Shopping Network and other video sales shows. Red, white, and blue figure prominently in set designs and borders framing the television screen. The Home Shopping Network presents its authorities in an office conspicuously adorned with a picture of the Statue of Liberty.[21] Yet the messages that the Home Shopping Network sends its customers—that you can buy as much speech as you can afford, that you are recognized by others in accordance with your capacity to consume—do much to subvert the connection between capitalism and democracy on which this semiotic identification depends.

The Art of Consumption and the Consumption of Art

The recognition of consumption as an act of representation, of commodities as signs, already revealed in popular practice, has also made itself visible in the works and criticism of high art. Picasso, who came, for a time, to represent the myth of art as Einstein represented the myth of science, was reported to use his work as currency, dashing off a quick drawing on a check or a napkin to pay for a lunch or settle a bill. Such actions could, however, be accommodated within the romantic myth of the artist. Picasso could be read as displaying a kind of romantic excess, a glorious magnanimity, in giving a priceless piece of art when money was demanded. The old stories of paintings bought for nothing from starving artists to be sold for millions later informed this interpretation of the exchange. Andy Warhol was more difficult to accommodate within the myth.

Art had been a commodity for centuries.[22] Despite this, the affirmation of art as a commodity took on the force of revelation in late twentieth century America. The subversion of the distinctions between art and other commodities was read as radical iconoclasm. The most notorious and hence the most effective of these subversions were Warhol's. Warhol's famous, or still, in some circles, infamous, painting of a Campbell's Soup can, propelled both the artist and the subject into the forefront of cultural criticism and popular debate. Warhol's work has a fine and informative ambivalence. His unabashed presentation of a commodity in the guise of art is (as he frankly pointed out) a presentation of art as a commodity. The Campbell's Soup can was, moreover, mass-produced: by Campbell's and by Warhol. Warhol simultaneously assaulted the division between high and popular culture, the identification of singularity with authenticity and value, the distinction between artist and manufacturer and between commodities and art. This tangle of critique, spoof, play, treatise, and question was to be extensively elaborated. Warhol's Factory presented art as a commodity, often a mass-manufactured commodity. His series of altered appropriations from news features (*Red Race Riot, Orange Disaster*) transforms the mass-manufactured image into art, even as it suggests the artfulness of that supposedly objective medium. His windows for Bonwit's blurred the boundary between art and advertisement. His altered appropriations of the features of celebrities (Marilyn Monroe, Jacqueline Kennedy, Mao, Elizabeth Taylor) celebrate the commodification of the self, a practice he engaged in on his own behalf with considerable success. The much-discussed posthumous sale of his effects was a fitting coda to his work.

By employing techniques of mass production, Warhol challenged the notion that singularity was essential to works of art. The broader significance of this challenge is evident in the name Warhol gave his studio, *the Factory*. The naming of the Factory simultaneously defied both the distinction between art and mass production, and the adulation of the artist as individual.

Warhol's appropriation of commonplace images, drawn from mass-produced commodities, ruptures the identification of the beautiful with the rare, of scarcity with value. A Campbell's Soup can in the grocery was a commodity. Represented in a two-dimensional form, in the context of gallery and museum, it became art. The transmutation revealed the alterations effected by the act of representation, the ascendancy of form over content. Yet it also conveyed a message with a readily accessible political import: context determines value. Value is arbitrarily raised or lowered by placement in the social order. With this, the political neutrality of the market was cast into question. It no longer appeared as an impersonal, disinterested, extracultural force but rather as a mechanism governed by the hierarchies operative in the political culture.

Warhol's appropriation of commercial images challenged the myth of individualism by mimicking one of its paradigmatic figures. The image of the willful artist, independent of technology, of bosses, of economic structures, of received opinion, impelled by private passions, singular in his (invariably his) genius, idiosyncratic in his dress and manners, was undermined by Warhol even as he exploited it. Despite the emergence and integration into the canon of Georgia O'Keeffe, Helen Frankenthaler, Louise Nevelson, and other women, the figure of the artist continued to be gendered male. He remained in the romantic mold of the wholly independent artist, whose ruthless selfishness, cruelty, and irresponsibility were the marks of genius. Warhol's Factory, and his appropriation of commercial images, presented the artist as dependent: on technology, on commerce, on the labor—and the ideas—of others. Warhol's exaggerated idiosyncracy presented idiosyncracy as a pose. His bald-faced self-construction, his seeking after celebrity and celebrities, presented the artist as product and commodity. The 1975 paperback edition of *The Philosophy of Andy Warhol* makes this argument visually, with great economy. The book is a commodity. The Campbell's design now signifies not only soup but Warhol and in this conflation marks both artist and product as commodities.[23]

Warhol's artistic recognition of the self as product and commodity issued in a fascination with shopping and a preoccupation with celebrity and celebrities.[24] Celebrity reveals itself in Warhol's work as a species of supplementarity. Celebrity presents itself as a simple addition, a cultural recognition or attribution of value. This ostensibly dependent attribution could, however, come to replace or overwhelm all others in the determination of identity. The emergence of a category of "celebrities" made this apparent. Anyone who ever looked at a tabloid or watched a television game show can name a series of people known to them simply as celebrities: Zsa Zsa Gabor, Orson Bean, Kitty Carlisle, Vanna White.

Warhol's series of celebrities captures several aspects of this process. The process of manufacture appears in the medium and the multiplication of the image. The transformative addition of celebrity appears in the color overlays, which simultaneously exaggerate and erase the features of the subject of the portrait. His choice of Marilyn Monroe invites a reading of celebrity as supplementarity, for her suicide offered a stark instance of erasure and replacement of the person by celebrity.

The appropriation of the mass-manufactured and the everyday figures in the works of Jasper Johns, Larry Rivers, Robert Rauschenberg, Tom Wesselmann, Claes Oldenburg, Jim Dine, and a host of others. Roy Lichtenstein adopted the idiom as well as the referents of mass culture in his appropriations of the comic book. Oldenburg's huge sculptures, a clothespin, a toothpaste tube, a baseball bat, effect the apotheosis of the everyday. His presentation of a toilet as a piece of art not only asserts, as Warhol, Duchamp, and others did before him, the importance of context in the meaning of an object, it also seems to sacralize the profane.

Johns performed the converse operation in his representations of the American flag: profaning the sacred. Johns presented the flag as a composition, ignoring its political and historical referents. The painterliness of Johns's works, and their conspicuous recognition of the painting as surface, aid the denial of the flag's signifying role.

Rivers, whose transmutations of history are mentioned earlier, was also engaged in deliberate transgressions of the boundaries between art and commodities. History, art and commodities, language and painting are inextricably entangled in the array of images in *French Money, Dutch Masters,* and *Dutch Masters Corona.*

Some of the most valuable commentaries on consumption are evident in those artistic works that came to be called Happenings. The Happening was a multimedia production invariably involving performances by artist and audience. Happenings combined seemingly unrelated actions and objects. Susan Sontag calls it "the art of radical juxtaposition." "The Happening," Sontag writes, "has no plot, though it is an action." It "is always in the present tense . . . one cannot hold on to a Happening." [25]

Like certain of those who produced and participated in the Happenings, Sontag mistakes this ephemerality for an escape from the routine world of commodities and consumption. The Happening, she argues, is not a commodity because it is "consumed on the premises." So is a hot dog. What distinguished the Happening was not the rapidity with which it was consumed, nor an exemption from the status of a commodity, but rather the exaltation of the ephemeral that informed its production. The ethos of the Happening is reminiscent of the Japanese concept of an apprehension of beauty dependent on its ephemerality: *aware.* As Alexandre Kojève observes, after Hegel, after Nietzsche, we are becoming steadily more Japanese. [26]

Because it was the experience that constituted the Happening, Happenings more nearly approached pure consumption. They were not, however, exempt from the effects of the process of their production or from the hierarchies these processes created. The Happening did succeed in rupturing the conventional boundaries of a work of art, in time and space. It did not, as was sometimes asserted, succeed in erasing the division between artist and viewer, producer and consumer. The viewers were indeed transformed into participants, but this transformation conferred upon them less the character of a collective artist than that of an additional resource. They provided the material on which the artist worked. Their participation, though it altered, even determined, the composition of the final work, conferred on them an authority equivalent to that of the materials whose features similarly constrained the artist. They did not escape the hierarchical relation that elevates the artist over the viewers and the work. The disparity between the authority of the artist and that of the participants in the Happening was not confined to their abstract status. Sontag notes the tendency of artists producing Happenings to "tease and abuse the audience," activities that enabled the artist—and obliged the audience—to experience this difference in authority directly.

The Happening transgressed the boundaries dividing artists from their material and, to a much smaller extent, those dividing artists and spectators in the process of production. More significantly, it diminished the practical distance between consumption and production. The participants in the Happening were at once its material and its consumers, and the time of production appeared as the time of consumption, though the work was constituted, in large part, by the artist before being cast in flesh. The "new art" and "new sensibility" that emerged in the 1960s were not, therefore, quite as insurrectionary as their proponents claimed. In recognizing that meaning is determined in consumption, and exploiting this type of authority in the creation of new works, the new art made a longstanding, but implicit and unconscious, American practice self-conscious and explicit. It took that practice from the masses and the commonplace and endowed it with the prestige of elite artistic patronage. In the broader phenomenon, as in each instance of the

Happening, popular practice and mass culture became the material out of which a new art and a new sensibility were produced.

Eating in America

80   The commodities that answer fundamental needs are, ironically, those that most often serve as signs. Clothing, which considerations of climate alone would oblige one to wear in most of the United States most of the time, provides a language of its own in which one cannot merely speak but speak subtly: affirm and deny, mock, challenge, and qualify.

Food speaks subtly as well. It serves as a mode of self-constitution, in which we challenge the ability of nature to give us our just deserts. We can speak—all the better with our mouths full—of our inclusion in nature or our conquest of nature, of our ability to impose our will upon our bodies or our attentiveness to their requirements. We can align ourselves with tradition, diversely understood, with modernity or postmodernity. Because food is the means for self-constitution in the simplest sense, it speaks directly to issues of identity. Among the clearest texts food offers are those that speak of ethnicity.

The first and clearest text on ethnicity is that inscribed in the distinction between "food" and "ethnic food." People eat food; "ethnics" eat ethnic food. Written into this distinction is the assumption that Americans are a people without culture, prior to it. It is the expression, in one aspect of everyday life, of the belief that "in the beginning all the world was America." Our food is not marked as culturally specific. Everyone can eat our food. Like most cultures, we regard our customary dishes, flavor preferences, and ordering of foods—eating sweets for breakfast and dessert and not eating insects at all—as natural. We differ from some in our expectation that anyone can eat and enjoy it, that it requires no genetic constitution, no training, no special, ethnically specific discernment (whether acquired by birth or training) to appreciate it. Except for a few intrepid bodies, we tend to regard our food as "just plain food," something that sustains life fairly pleasurably. If one wants to stimulate the palate, to eat for aesthetics, one eats from another cuisine. Even those interested in American cooking as an art form tend to differentiate their dishes (even versions of traditional dishes) from "regular food." Aesthetic preoccupation with food at this level (rather than the "M'm! M'm! Good!" of Campbell's Soup) is popularly regarded as something of an affectation.

The designation of some foods as ethnic foods and others as food enables one to read texts on assimilation and ethnicity on the grocery shelves. In Princeton, New Jersey, South Bend, Indiana, and in most of Chicago, there is one kind of salsa, or perhaps two (hot and mild), and salsa is most likely to be found in the ethnic foods sections. In Austin, there are four or five at any grocery, fresh and canned, in the refrigerator section and on the shelves. Salsa, for Texans, is just food. To accompany it they have five or six kinds of tortilla chips, three locally made, including black bean, sesame blue corn, and lime and chile, none of which are to be found in the ethnic foods section. The produce department will have black beans and pinto beans in bulk, chile pods, tomatillos, and anaheim, poblano, and serrano peppers. In New Jersey, the deli section has capicolla, mortadella, prosciutto, and often fresh mozzarella, but chile pods, if they appear at all, appear as a means of home decoration. Cilantro, right next to the parsley in Texas, can be found in Princeton only one day a week at the Asian grocery. It never made it to the Foodtown.

Reading the grocery in any town is informative for anyone who wants to know which ethnicities are represented there, their degree of assimilation, and whether or not they are welcome. It also provides a commentary on the character of assimilation in America. Mexican food, for example, is available in three forms in Austin. There are foods recognized here and elsewhere as Mexican that nevertheless appear simply as food: lime and chile chips, cilantro, and the variety of peppers. There are foods that retain their foreign flavor and consequently appear in the ethnic foods section—types of mole, for example, shelved just above the elaborately decorated devotional candles. Finally, there are "Mexican" foods that are seen as Mexican in a quite different sense: Lawry's Taco Seasoning, Fritos, Nacho Cheese Doritos, and the Mexican Hamburger

Helper. Foods of this sort offer a disturbing commentary on assimilation. While they appear to preserve difference, they effectively erase it.

Ethnic foods, in the latter two cases, are a supplement. Like ethnicity itself, they are understood as something extra that is added to people who are, after all, "all the same under the skin." In the first of these, ethnicity is clearly an addendum, set apart in the grocery, marked as foreign. In the second, ethnicity has become an additive. In each case, the construction of ethnicity as discrete and isolable marks its replacement in the constitution of identity.

Eating as a Metaphor

The use of eating as a metaphor for aggression, assimilation, power, and inclusion is a commonplace in American political culture, from the early years of the republic to the present. The grandiose pronouncements of Davy Crockett echo in the words of Robert Coover's Uncle Sam. "Who-Whoo-Whoop! Who'll come gouge with me? Who'll come bite with me? . . . I can ride a flash of lightnin', catch a thunderbolt in my fist, swaller niggers whole, raw or cooked . . . I am feeling awesome wolfy about the head and shoulders." [27] Eating is power in America. The passion for an expansive identity, and the attendant fear of consuming the poisonous or the indigestible, animate Americans of the twentieth century as they echo the words of Americans of the nineteenth.

The Fourth of July is often celebrated these days as a festival of consumption. After the parade down Main Street, and before the fireworks, the citizenry that once regaled itself with oratory now displays its national oral prowess on a more individual level. In streets and malls, parks and parking lots, one will find large companies of tables and tents, and within them a vast array of foods, representing the immigrant nationalities that settled in the area. In the Midwest, the Wisconsin fried cheese truck settles in next to the stand selling Vietnamese egg rolls. There are kolachkis and wontons, pirogi, bagels and calzone, elephant ears and corn dogs, greens, fajitas, and, if you are fortunate, some foreign food that you have never seen. People move from one tent to the next, eating tacos and tortoni, tasting Jamaican stews and Thai noodles, jambalaya and sopa-pillas. They eat not from one region but from many, not only of the foods they know but of those they do not, not only of the foods of their immigrant ancestors but from the foods of all who came to America.

In these Fourth of July celebrations, Americans reenact the constitution of the American people. They take the foreign within their boundaries and make it their own. In this festive gesture they affirm the ability of America to accommodate di-versity, to encompass all nationalities in one. These festivals of eating mark ethnic diversity as a source of nourishment and pleasure. We eat these diverse foods, grow, and prosper. The nation that has absorbed these diverse immigrants prospers as well, nourished by their contributions to the body politic. The more diverse the foods, and the more exotic they are, the more pleasure we have at the festival. We delight in the display and the consumption of difference. This ethnic diversity presents it-self as virtually unlimited choice—overcoming time and dis-tance. You can have it all, and you can have it here, in your own backyard. Here, ethnicity—like eating itself—is a choice, not a necessity. You can eat the foods of your ancestors if you choose, and if you don't, you can choose another. Neither history nor convention binds you. Ethnicity becomes—at least for the mo-ment—a matter of election.

Each eater, in these festivals of self-constitution, affirms an individual capacity to accommodate cultural difference. Each, like Walt Whitman, contains multitudes. Yet on what terms? These festivals, which I have read thus far as celebrations of cultural difference and ethnic diversity, invite other readings. This silent, multivocal act of eating affirms the ability of the one who eats to act at one moment as an African-American, at an-other as a Polish-American. It persuades us that we are figura-tively as well as literally open to this wide diversity of cultures, that we can "take them in." We may ourselves be taken in by this enacted affirmation of our ability to comprehend cultures.

The silent affirmation of our singular (and collective) abil-ity to take something from the Italians, and something from the Japanese, and make them part of a whole accords to the liberal notion of a self with an essential core, always altering, but never essentially altered by, that which is absorbed. Other ways of eating ethnic food suggest a different capacity to alter identity at will and, preserving difference, to become at one moment one identity, at another, another.

The reading of the consumption of ethnic foods as a means of constituting oneself, for a moment, as Chinese or Mexican or Cajun is supported by the conventions of dining in an ethnic restaurant. One who goes out to eat at an ethnic restaurant experiences not simply a change of food but a change of scene. Chinese restaurants are likely to have dragons on the outside, some architectural evocations of the Chinese style, and, within, paintings on silk or heavily carved screens. It is thought to be good form to eat (or try to eat) with chopsticks. In a Mexican restaurant, one may be served on earthenware pottery from Mexico, and the rooms will be decorated by pinatas, cut paper banners, or cut tin ornaments. There may be live or recorded Mexican music, and the waiters are likely to wear some element of Mexican dress. Insofar as the resources of restaurant and customer permit, the customers not only eat Mexican or Chinese food, they eat it as if they were in Mexico or China, as if they were Mexican or Chinese.

The experience of eating is not always presented, however, as if it could produce a momentary adoption of another identity. The reading that identifies eating as the capacity to consume something of another identity without being altered oneself also shows itself in common practices and commodities, for example, in fast-food establishments. Taco Bell, Taco Tio, Taco Pronto, and a host of others offer food identified with Mexico in a context the whole world knows as American. Many of the Greek restaurants of Chicago offer souvlakia, gyros, dolmas, and baklava, along with meatloaf, french fries, fried chicken, and cheeseburgers in an atmosphere more reminiscent of diners than Athens or Delphi or Chicago's Greektown. The presentation of Greek foods in an American context offers not an experience of exotic identity but an affirmation of assimilation.

The silent, multivocal act of eating also offers several commentaries—both critical and celebratory—on the process of Americanization. Ethnic differences are celebrated in eating. The presence of difference is the presence of choice; the experience of difference is the experience of freedom, pleasure, and self-constitution. Yet all differences are erased in digestion.

The variety of things that enter are transmuted into one all-absorbing whole. The body politic that took in these differences absorbs and assimilates them to itself. Read in this way, eating and the history of immigration it enacts appear as the violent erasure of difference, as the conquest rather than the comprehension of ethnicity.

Much would be lost if we were to indulge the desire to de- **85** cide between these diverse readings. The easy reconciliation opposing views find in a single practice suggests not that we should find error in one interpretation but that we should find truths in the contradictions of the practice.

Consumption as Critique

The practices of consumption in America reveal in practice the contradictions entailed in the idea of representation. The capacity to cast oneself, or some aspects of oneself, into another material form (a book, a hat, a Constitution, or one's elected representative) permits people to become visible, present, and communicative when they might otherwise be absent, silent, or dead. Yet it subjects those who avail themselves of it to the constraints entailed in the forms they choose. They are limited in their choices to what has been chosen for them. Those who express themselves through commodities also find that this form of self-expression, this means of public discourse, does not permit them equal access to speech nor does it permit them to speak to one another as equals. The practices of consumption in America enact ideas central to liberalism: that choice is freedom and free choice evidence of consent, that people exercise authority in the selection of representatives and representations of themselves, and that the representation does not replace but instead extends the self.

The presence of these principles in every crevice of American life—from high art to shopping—shows their breadth and commonalty. The presence of these principles in the most mundane aspects of American life—eating and dressing—shows the depth and intensity of their constitutive power. Yet these practices put into question the very principles they put into practice. They reveal coercion in the context of choice. They show the power of the representation to overcome that which it purports to represent. The translation of the canonical texts into the quotidian practices of liberalism shows the theory's power, and its failings. The questions that these practices have put to theory show the method and the direction of a continuing constitutional enterprise.

THREE

The President as Sign

IN THE CONTEMPORARY INTELLECTUAL LITERATURES of the American regime, the presidency figures as an institution, the President as a political actor. In the practices of popular culture, as in an older literature, the President is seen to serve another purpose. Tocqueville observes, in the early years of the Republic, that the primacy of the majority in America subordinated the President's institutional function to his role as sign.[1]

In the United States as elsewhere parties feel the need to rally around one man in order more easily to make themselves understood by the crowd. Generally, therefore, they use the Presidential candidate's name as a symbol; in him they personify their theories. Hence the parties have a great interest in winning the election, not so much to make their doctrines triumph by the President-elect's help as to show, by his election, that their doctrines have gained majority.[2]

The President's representative function is, in Tocqueville's understanding, first semiotic, and only secondarily executive. The President does not serve simply as the executive of the popular will expressed through legislation. Rather, the President serves first as a symbol and, secondly, as rhetorical strategy.

Tocqueville's discerning construction recognizes the ambivalence of Presidential authority. The President is made a symbol through election: the electorate not only authorizes rule, it authors significance as well. Tocqueville also suggests, obliquely, that the President is the creature and creation of the party. The candidate serves these as a rhetorical strategy; "in him they personify their theories," in order to make themselves more easily understood by the masses. This last, and least noted, of presidential functions has become conspicuous in American political culture.

The President represents, in an instance of official multivocality, the nation, the government, the executive branch, and (as Tocqueville observes) the triumphant party. The President who meets and negotiates with foreign heads of state, who attends the funerals of soldiers and astronauts, who lights the Christmas tree and throws out the first ball, and who (very occasionally) casts into words the incandescent spirit of a people represents the nation. Those who directed their protests against the war in Vietnam to Presidents Johnson and Nixon took them as representative of the government that had embroiled the nation in that war. At such moments the President represents not the nation but the government. In messages to Congress, in proposing (and vetoing) legislation, in responding to (or contesting) congressional requests for information, the President represents the executive branch. These diverse representations become confounded with, and inflected by, one another. All are colored by the recognition of the President as representative of partisan triumph.

Winning an election is a victory in itself. The enthusiasm with which people await and greet and celebrate their candidate's triumph is not the measured satisfaction of those who have acquired a particularly useful instrument. They have won, and they will retain that victory if Congress blocks the reforms they desire, or their candidate, now President, fails to pursue them. Their enthusiasm is not, however, merely the joy that might accompany the winning of any game played for high stakes. It is a recognition of the authority of representation.

Elections leave a mark on history. They divide time into periods. By this victory alone, candidate and party write history. In doing so they do more than inscribe their names. They assert, perhaps counter to other evidence, the continuance or interruption of periods of party ascendancy. They provide the markers from which those inclined to see cycles in American politics will fashion their theories. Winning an election confers not only a partial authority over legislation, it confers a partial, but nevertheless significant, authority over history. Electoral triumph may, as Tocqueville observes, indicate that a particular doctrine has won the endorsement of a majority. Often it does not. The procedures that cull out candidates from the people, that govern campaigns and elections (including the role of the electoral college) and the low levels of voting in many elections, may give the victory to one who lacks the support of a majority. The victor can be sure, at best, only of having won a majority of those who voted.[3] A President who wins with that 60 percent which is now called a landslide in an election where turnout is lower than 60 percent, and the proportion of registered to eligible voters still less, would seem to possess only a tenuous mandate. Yet such candidates take office with confidence. They rely on the semiotic power of the victory itself.

89

The recognition that such victories transcend their numbers has not been lost on Americans. Those who rejoice at the victory or grieve at the defeat of their candidates know it. Perhaps the best description of the phenomenon—and, though the terms are not overtly analytic, the most carefully articulated analysis—is given by Vachel Lindsay in his account of the election of 1896. Lindsay's account conveys the semiotic and historical significance of the election. William Jennings Bryan's defeat was not merely the defeat of a candidate, it was the "defeat of the wheat . . . defeat of my boyhood, defeat of my dream." McKinley's victory was

> Victory of letterfiles
> And plutocrats in miles
> . . . .
> Victory of custodians
> Plymouth Rock
> And all that inbred landlord stock.
> Victory of the neat.[4]

The historical authority of elections derives in large part from the structure of the office and the electoral process. The presidency is a single office. One party will lose the election, and another will win. With that victory, the winning party erases its opponents. The candidate who wins with 60 percent of the vote is said to have a mandate. It is not said, though it might be true, that such a candidate has 40 percent of the voters in opposition.

Realignments are effected not only by demographic changes in the electorate that issue in different configurations of interests and hence of ideologies. They also depend for their accomplishment on changes in signification. An altered signification of already present divisions in the electorate changes the meaning of those divisions and prompts changes in party affiliation. One aspect of this change is effected by a change in the President as signifier. The Democratic party of Jackson was not, despite the protests of its adherents and considerable doctrinal constancy, the Democratic party of Jefferson; the party of Johnson was not the party of Lincoln—or Kennedy. Changing the party's representative changes the meaning of the party.

This change secures those that made it possible, simultaneously effecting and marking them. Revaluations are not peculiar to critical elections and periods of radical realignment. They are entailed in the act of representation. They occur in each selection of a candidate, in each campaign (and, of course, in acts of representation beyond these). Each representative (each representation) presents, as sign, "a kind of knowledge, a past, a memory, a comparative order of facts, ideas, decisions" in addition to the party doctrines each partisan candidate signifies.[5] By altering the mythic context and primary referents of the political discourse, a successful candidate may alter not only the meaning of the party but the meaning of the rival, the rival's party, and the nation that each endeavors to represent.

A series of prior confrontations, challenges to the meaning of the parties and their opposition, are crystallized, made material, made objective, in a change in party leadership. These confrontations and challenges are not confined to state structures, to offices, or to the powerful. As Gayatri Chakravorty Spivak observes, the relatively unremarked activities of the subaltern effect the alterations of political meanings, the expansions and contractions of the political field, on which institutional realignments depend, and which they mark. The person, the body, the image, that serves as a sign stands at the nexus of a plethora of networks of meaning (histories, social structures, etc.) that are themselves interrelated. Signification is thus neither simple nor arbitrary. As signifier the President calls up not only the American nation, the government, the executive branch, and the triumphant party (already a rich—and variable—assemblage of images) but the mythic and historical associations that attach to the office and to its past and present occupants. The presidency comprises a collection of associations that includes "the American Dream," war powers, impeachment, and assassination. Each connotation is embedded in a historical context that is also available in the image. Impeachment recalls Andrew Johnson and Richard Nixon, assassination Lincoln and Kennedy. The seemingly static singularity of the·sign brings history with it, a history that may serve as a standard or a source of alternatives. The personal traits and history—the image—of each occupant of the office carries connotations of its own. Kennedy's image called up the complex, contradictory connotations of Camelot and Catholicism, continental chic and touch football, the Ivy League and the Boston Irish, privilege and exclusion. Sign and image carry their subversion in themselves. Nixon's invocations of Lincoln called up not only Lincoln's tragedy but his Civil War, not only Lincoln's troubles with the press but his successor's impeachment by the Congress. Truman's plain midwestern democracy called up the aristocracy of his predecessor, and Jackson's rambunctious frontier image was shadowed by the austere intellectualism of rival John Quincy Adams.

The availability of this richness of reference is of profound importance for political discourse. As Barthes observes, it nourishes the signification, acting as "an instantaneous reserve of history, a tamed richness which it is possible to call and dismiss in a sort of rapid alternation."[6] Embedded in that already-established, already-understood, history, the image appears natural and unmediated, without an ideology, an impression enhanced by visual media. The President appears to us as a person, an embodied individual presence whom we see directly. Yet that person is veiled from us by history and the presidential office. The natural bodily singularity of the person is supplemented by the plurality of referents in the image of the President.

91

The plurality of referents makes possible a variety of strategies in the employment of, and response to, this act of signification. The histories the referents carry with them renders strategies vulnerable, however, for though they are commonly motivated by a specific rhetorical and ideological intent, they supply both the motive for subversion and the means to attempt it. Consider the face of a presidential candidate. This image on a campaign poster serves as a rallying point for supporters and as the signifier of a platform of policy proposals and issue operations. The same image, however, can be made into a rubber mask. The first signification entailed the use of a medium associated with acclamation, the second a medium evocative of ridicule.[7]

The difference context makes is more profoundly, though more discreetly, evident in Lincoln. The passage of nearly one hundred years between Lincoln's assassination and the March on Washington, the nationalization of American allegiance in those years, the absence of threats to the Union, and the continued presence of the race issue had muted praise of Lincoln as "Savior of the Union" and forged an enduring and profoundly meaningful association between the name of Lincoln and the Emancipation Proclamation. The name of the proclamation (rather than its text) allied to the name of a man whose expressed opinions on black equality were rather more ambiguous than the honorific "the Great Emancipator" implies made it possible, indeed necessary, that Martin Luther King, Jr., in his speech at the Lincoln Memorial would evoke a posthumous endorsement in Lincoln's name. Because second order signs, like Lincoln, entail references to a variety of semiotic systems and political structures, their meaning may be considerably altered by changes in their historical-political context. Such changes are important in permitting, or precluding, rhetorical strategies employing the President as sign. They are interesting in part because they enable one to map out the reconstitution of the past by the present.

The peculiar utility of the concept of President as sign is not merely in the distinction it makes between the President as an individual—possessed of a body with peculiar traits, a mind with idiosyncratic opinions, embedded in a particular social and historical context with attendant distinctions of occupation, ethnicity, religion, and other traits—and the President as the holder of an office. This distinction does not belong to semiotics. It has perhaps its most articulate exposition in Max Weber's writings on bureaucracy and has figured in juridical and philosophical discussions of the paradoxes of leadership at least since Elizabethan writings on "the king's two bodies." [8] Semiotics enables us to recognize that this separation is imperfect. The signifier and the signified are finally inseparable in the sign. Their interdependence is entailed in the concept of representation. When we recognize that the office is distinct from its occupant, we recognize its abstract character. We fail to remember that the form a representation takes affects its meaning and significance. All offices undergo a transubstantiation when they are occupied.

The process of election itself obliges us to notice that the personal traits, private character, and historical circumstances of the President contribute as much to the President's authority as does the office. What tends to go unnoticed is the manner in which particular occupants shape the meaning—as well as the function—of the offices they occupy. In doing so, subsequent occupants acquire not only authority over the office but over the meaning and significance of those who preceded them. The historical authority exercised by—and upon—Franklin Roosevelt and Reagan illustrates the variety of representative strategies made available to Presidents through the interplay of signifier and signified in the sign. In their form, these examples illustrate the strategic consequences of signification. In their content, they illuminate elements of the network of meaning that constitutes American political culture. Taken together, they illustrate the complex, reciprocally constitutive relation of present and past.

Reagan

Reagan presents an inviting object for semiotic analysis. His presidency, and his life as he reads it, possess a profoundly representative character. No novelty, but some importance, remains in the observation that Reagan effectively employed the skills of an actor in the roles of candidate and President. These skills consist of the use of a complex lexicon of words and gestures evocative, in this case, of a mythic American identity and conception of leadership. Reagan's reading of his life, presented in his autobiographical productions (my cinematic language here echoes Reagan's own) and in the autobiographical anecdotes that figured prominently in his public statements, presents that life as representative not only of Walt Whitman's "divine average" but also of American nationality in its mythic expression and in the course of its contemporary development.[9] Reagan is born blazoned with the national colors. The causes and course of his disillusionment with Roosevelt represent the course of national development as he reads—and writes—it.

In 1965, while campaigning for governor, and the willing object of a "draft Reagan" campaign for the Republican presidential nomination, Reagan published an autobiography. Autobiographies as campaign documents are hardly novelties on the political scene. Davy Crockett's senatorial campaign produced an early and enduring example of the genre. They are interesting, in part, because of the frequency with which they appear and the purposes they serve in the political process. They are deliberate attempts to establish the candidate's credentials as leader and representative, not according to minimal constitutional standards, or to those standards that party ideology or legal rational principles would dictate, but rather according to the political culture's mythology of leadership and national character. They impose on selected incidents in the candidate's life, and on traits ascribed to the candidate, a reading that is calculated to accord with prevailing notions of "leader" and "representative."

Reagan begins his autobiography with his birth. "My face was blue from screaming, my bottom was red from whacking, and my father claimed afterward that he was white when he said shakily 'For such a little bit of a fat Dutchman he makes a hell of a lot of noise.' "[10] Having thus designated the incident and the traits to be recognized, he offers an interpretation. He has always been fond, he writes, of the colors exhibited on that occasion. At the very outset of the narrative Reagan presents himself as the sign of nationality, not merely "flying the flag" but "showing his true colors," exhibiting an innate rather than conventional patriotism and identifying himself with the most arbitrary and least ambiguous sign of nationality, the flag.

In this passage Reagan also reveals his relation to a complex of corporeal metaphors, a network that binds together capitalism and America's imperial destiny, commerce, conquest, and corporations. In his expressions of, and self-construction within, this complex of corporeal metaphors Reagan evinces the continued capacity of Western mythology to legitimate, and contributes to its perpetuation—albeit in a necessarily altered form.

Reagan prides himself, in the autobiography, on exhibiting in infancy a trait peculiar to the West: extraordinary oral prowess. The mythic Westerner had an "alligator grin . . . that made 'em all hold onto their hair for fear it would fly out." He could "laugh a horse blind," and he (or she, for the women were similarly gifted) had "teeth like nails." Crockett personified the mythic ·Westerner to his generation. Like Crockett, Reagan exploited Western mythology for political advantage, presenting himself as the incarnation of this still popular archetype. Reagan's vociferous infant screams marked the inauguration of those oral capacities that would later aid in prodigious feats of consumption. After he got to be so great a speechifier and was sent to the presidency, Reagan would do his eating off $952-a-place-setting china, surpassing Crockett in the most rantankerous manner. He consumed more on the plates alone than Crockett could by filling them. Reagan also claimed, like Crockett, to exhibit superhuman powers in his more material feats of ingestion. *Time* reports that "at one session he fingered a jelly bean, joked, "They tell me the purple ones are poison," then nonchalantly popped it into his mouth.[11]

Crockett's grins and Reagan's screaming, Crockett's appetite and Reagan's china, could figure merely as coincidental and insignificant instances of things oral were it not for their metaphoric significance. Crockett's mythic consumption—of Indians, Yankees, "bar," pork steak, spike nails, and whiskey in prodigious quantities—is not, of course, an accurate account of antebellum appetites. It follows from a characteristically Western identification of the individual with the nation. America was referred to, in that period, as "a great land animal," "a young and growing country" that, as Michael Rogin remarks, was thought to expand by "swallowing territory." Westerners, then, were the mouth of the nation, that part of it that initiated expansion, absorbing the territory that would henceforth be incorporated into the nation. The Westerner's mythic capacity for consumption thus represents an assertion of the Western capacity to take in territory and expand the nation. Western eating was Western conquest.[12]

The aggressive character of Western eating is evident in Crockett's appetites. He is cannibalistic, eating Yankees and Indians just as the Western territories swallowed up individual representatives of those cultural subgroups. Reagan presents himself as equally oral, equally aggressive. His infant screaming, that "hell of a lot of noise" that he contrasts with his (Democratic) father's weakness, helps transform him into a representation of America: red, white, and blue. Reagan's embodiment of America is manifested, however, in speech rather than in eating. Like the mythic Westerner who swallows "bars" and grins down hickory nuts, Reagan used his oral abilities to provide himself with sustenance. Like the Westerner who could swallow an Indian whole without choking and eat any man opposed to Jackson, Reagan fought his enemies with his mouth.

If eating to excess was the reason Crockett got to be so good a speechifier and was sent to Congress, speaking prodigiously—as sports announcer, actor, partisan activist in the Hollywood unions, and spokesman for General Electric—was the reason for Reagan's entry into politics. Indeed, his oratorical skill is frequently cited, by friend and foe alike, as the reason for his consequent political success.

The form of oral aggression thus differentiates Reagan from the Western model. At a deeper level, however, it becomes apparent that this seeming difference is merely the consequence of a more thorough identity. The oral aggression of the mythic Westerner is material; Reagan's was ideal. In the antebellum period, American expansion was territorial, and the Westerner identified himself with a materially expanding nation. At present, the extension of American dominion is identified with the extension of American influence, the triumph of American ideology. Like another mythic Westerner, Vachel Lindsay's Jackson, Reagan's foreign policy was directed to "making democrats of these / and Freedom's sons of Japanese."[13] Territorial expansion had been abandoned in favor of hegemony. What was sought was no longer land but influence, treaties, and alliances—written and spoken acknowledgments of an American imperium. It was appropriate, therefore, that speaking should replace eating as the metaphoric instrument of national expansion. The continued use of oral aggression reflected a continued preoccupation with the expansion of the nation, while the alternate method reflected a change in the mode and methods of national expansion.

Consumption, in the material sense, remains a compelling and popular metaphor in American political culture. We continue to expand through eating. Indices of national consumption are used as measures of economic health, along with the Gross National Product. Self-consciousness of America as a culture of production and consumption has resulted not in a diminution of eating metaphors but in their proliferation and refinement. They are less obtrusive. Economic language is so well established that the corporeal referents of *corporate, incorporation,* and *product* are rarely recognized.

The threat of being the consumed rather than the consumer also retains its place in American mythology. Westerners had feared Indian cannibalism. The *Crockett Almanacs* tell of Indians who threaten to drink the blood of settlers. Each confrontation of man and bear ends with one or the other as the meal. For Reagan and his staff, government was "like a baby, an alimentary canal with an appetite at one end and no sense of responsibility at the other. If you keep feeding it, we'll be up to our necks on something . . . oh yes. Debt." [14] In this passage, Reagan appears confident of his ability to control governmental appetite. Others evinced greater trepidation. "Do you realize the greed that came to the forefront?" David Stockman asked, "The hogs were really feeding." [15] While the Reagan administration endeavored to restrict governmental consumption, "all kinds of decisions made five, ten, fifteen years ago are coming back to bite us unexpectedly. Therefore in my judgement it will take three or four or five years to subdue it. Whether anyone can maintain the political momentum to fight the beast for that long I don't know." [16] There was only one way to win. There were "huge bites that would have to be taken out of Social Security. I mean really fierce, blood-and-guts stuff." [17]

Foreign affairs were also portrayed as conflicts in which one was either the eater or the eaten. Reagan warned, "like a ravening wolf, Castro's Cuba looks to peace-loving neighbors with hungry eyes and sharp teeth." [18] The greatest enemy, however, remained "the evil empire," the Soviet Union, whose ambition to incorporate additional territories and extend its influence was the principle target of Reagan's foreign policy. Reagan's greatest enemy, like Crockett's, was the bear.

The mythic battle between man and bear has been much altered in its representations. Crockett battled the bear. Jacksonian America seized on the Crockett myth as a representation of the national battle against the natural forces that threatened the expanding frontier. In later decades the battle for territory became a battle for influence; once material conflicts became not only ideologized but abstract, idealized. The expansion of American dominion was still regarded as intrinsically desirable, and the battle with the bear continued, in an altered form. A once physical conflict was replaced—or, rather, represented—by conflict in speech. The signification of a feared physical conflict simultaneously replaced and perpetuated it. This signified conflict, this "war of words" as the press called it, was one in which Reagan could represent himself as an adept combatant.

In the midst of what he characterizes as the first engagement in his personal war against communism, Reagan belittled a Hollywood opponent with the phrase "he had been nowhere, even when we were fighting with the U.S.S.R. against Hitler." Here Reagan's identification of himself with the nation served simultaneously to reiterate his patriotism and to suggest that he, unlike his opponent, had active military experience in that conflict. This was, at best, an exaggeration. Reagan saw no action. His active duty was spent behind the desk and in the studio. He had, however, seen a good bit of action on the screen, as a navy flier and an RAF pilot, among other roles. Reagan's actual military career bore more than a family resemblance to his cinematic military service.

Reagan's military career was distinguished by his participation in "one of the better kept secrets of the war, ranking up with the atom bomb project." This was "a pure Hollywood product." Reagan and his colleagues constructed small-scale models of Tokyo and "other principal Japanese targets" and used these to film simulated bombing runs. These then served to brief bombing crews for the actual attack. Reagan dwelt at length on the verisimilitude of the simulated runs. "Even the generals," he writes, "were unable to pick out the scenes that were actually Tokyo, and tell them from the model." Bombing crews would sit in the theater viewing a simulation of a plane flying at thirty thousand feet. "Beneath them would be the Pacific, in the distance the hazy coastline." "My voice," Reagan recalls, "would be heard above the sound of plane motors." They would fly on, over "Japan," "right into the point where my voice said, 'Bombs away.'" [19]

Reagan's role in this project recapitulated his past and set the pattern for his future occupational history. He was the voice. As sports announcer he narrated conflicts on the football field; as the fictive leader of the cinematic bomb crew he described a simulated flight and ordered the dropping of imaginary bombs. The bomb runs that followed the simulation would reenact the fictive run that Reagan had narrated. His speech was thus not merely predictive—it was authoritative. The cinematic run signified an actual run to be accomplished in the future, through imitation of the signifier.

"Following each raid," Reagan writes, "recon planes would fly their film direct from Saipan to us so that we could burn out portions of our target scenes and put in the scars of the bombing." [20] A simulated route, a simulated target, simulated bombs, and a simulated route, a simulated target, simulated bombs, and a simulated devastation. Reagan was schooled in a war where scars are made on film and the dead are resurrected for the next take. It is not altogether surprising that Reagan should have jocularly conflated the war in the Pacific with conflicts in the Wild West. (His log for one night on duty—in Culver City—reads, "3 a.m.—Post attacked by three regiments of Japanese infantry. Led cavalry charge and repulsed enemy. Quiet resumed.")[21] Nor, given his occupational history, is it altogether surprising that Reagan should equate the war he fought on film with the war that other Americans fought in the flesh. What is surprising is that Americans should have concurred in these conflations, accepting without embarrassment or ridicule Reagan's identification with those who fought on the front lines in World War II, and praising his bravery with reference not merely to fictional cinematic heroes but to the actors who portrayed them. Thus Senator Alphonse D'Amato, praising Reagan's speech to Congress after the assassination attempt, said, "He out-Wayned John Wayne." [22]

As Senator D'Amato's praise suggests, this conflation of the cinematic signifier and the signified is not limited to Reagan as subject or as object. When Reagan urged a foe to "make my day," the phrase was ascribed not to the fictional Harry Callahan but to Clint Eastwood. Eastwood, like Wayne, has been identified with the characters he has portrayed. Like Reagan, he has parlayed a cinematic into a political career. In none of these cases, however, is the actor actually confused with the role. Those who ascribe Callahan's fictional traits to Eastwood would nevertheless identify the latter's occupation as "actor" rather than "policeman." What is at work here—and what was at work in Reagan's political persona—is neither delusion nor ignorance but something far more interesting.

Reagan's election, and the widespread support he maintained throughout his presidency, indicate that his public persona accorded well with American notions of the "leader" and "representative." Reagan's undistinguished military career is a matter of public record. His occupational history evinced none of the traits or experiences identified with leadership. Yet he laid claim to those traits and his claim was accepted. What Reagan revealed, and the American people recognized, was not his possession but his representation of the qualities of leadership. He was elected as signifier.

This disjunction is equally evident in another dimension of Reagan's presidency. Reagan presented himself as the advocate and champion of traditional values—the sanctity of the family, the primacy of religion. Many observed that much in Reagan's conduct belied this advocacy. He attended church rarely, he was divorced, and he saw his children and their children seldom. He denied, as signifier, the values he purported to signify.

Reagan's reputation was affected little, if at all, by these observations. There may be, of course, considerable appeal in the disjunction. Americans, like Reagan, may not practice what they preach. His lapses may thus have increased his evident likeness to the "divine average," whose conduct, like his own, fell short of its professed ideals.

The explanatory power of this argument of hypocrisy is,

however, insufficient. The "traditional family," "prayer in the schools," "the right to life," and other such utterances contain layer upon layer of signification. The argument of hypocrisy privileges one layer of meaning without attention to the relative importance of these layers in political discourse. These utterances signify not only—and often not primarily—an unambiguous and readily identified policy or set of policies but also constellations of values, myths, images, and political orientations that may be variously construed in different subcultures and different political contexts. An endorsement of any of these utterances may thus be an endorsement not (or not primarily) of the policy but rather of the position it represents.

These utterances with their richness of reference are recognized by those who hear and those who employ them as multivocal signs. Because they are so rich in referents, so full of meaning, they are not taken as prescribing a clear and unambiguous course. Rather they serve to locate those who employ them within the network of meaning that constitutes the culture. Reagan's vigorous defense of the "right to life" was thus less an indication of willingness to extend himself to ensure the passage of bills or amendments prohibiting abortion and more an indication of those segments of the culture with which he wished to align himself and whose mores he chose to endorse. His supporters could regard him as having kept the faith, whether or not he was successful in securing particular policy objectives, as long as he remained a representative of the values, images, and mores that the utterance "right to life" calls up in its adherents.

Horace Holley, in an early nineteenth century lecture given before Lafayette, argued that American language, unlike the languages of Europe, was language "in earnest," continually corrected and refined by "the consent of those who are deeply concerned to maintain its truth and significancy." [23] The examples of democratic speech offered by Reagan and, more profoundly, in the Constitution, would seem to indicate, on the contrary, a distinct lack of veracity. The American penchant for extravagant boasting and for tall tales also seems to contradict the earnestness claimed for democratic speech. Americans appear to put their faith in falsehoods.

This acceptance of the false for the true, of the actor not for the role but for the qualities portrayed, and of the representative for the represented is not gullibility. Rather it indicates an acceptance of the conventions that undergird legal rational authority and a credit economy, a people grown accustomed to signification. The prominence of false speech in American heroic mythology, however, suggests that Americans regard speech and other forms of signification as not merely abstract representations but as potentially authoritative. When Crockett declares that he will "eat any man opposed to Jackson," he signifies the intensity of his partisanship and his capacity to overwhelm the opposition, not his prandial intentions.

The acceptance of claims about the powers of the self when they are manifestly at variance with objective reality is one indication of the primacy of subjectivity. The Westerner's boast, Reagan's representations of himself as war veteran and family man, and other such may be interpreted by those who hear them as expressions of an inner state that is regarded as telling one more about the speaker than the "facts" do. The constitutional structure of the American regime and American mythic history likewise assert that "wishing will make it so." Horatio Alger stories and the mythic account of Lincoln's rise from log cabin to the presidency, of Edison's inventions, of Carnegie's rise to wealth, and of Lindbergh's trans-Atlantic crossing assert the invincibility and creative capacities of individuals. The mythic accounts of Manifest Destiny, of America's role in the two world wars, and the sophistication and variety of American technology, sending a man to the moon and creating a government by an act of will, assert the collective invincibility of the people and the creative capacity of the popular will. Americans, collectively and individually, are successfully engaged in securing the conquest of nature by will.

Franklin Roosevelt

The Great Depression, arriving hard on the heels of the seemingly limitless prosperity of the 1920s, gave the lie to both these elements of the American faith. Confidence in credit, in the value of paper money, paper stocks, paper contracts, was swept away like the refuse of a ticker tape parade, or the leavings of a day on the trading floor. At the same moment, the seemingly illimitable expansion of the American economy, its vast industrial enterprises endlessly producing technological wonders, ground to a halt. Banks collapsed, homes were lost, farms auctioned off, and in the West the dust bowl reclaimed acre after acre of the land nature had lost to human will. In the midst of this the nation gave itself over to the rule of a cripple. "The only thing we have to fear," Roosevelt told them, "is fear itself."

This spoken reaffirmation of the primacy of subjectivity and the power of the will from a man whose body offered a seemingly decisive refutation marked the triumph of individual will and inaugurated the resurrection of the collective's faith in its own omnipotence.

Roosevelt has been given much credit in recent years for the dexterity with which he disguised his paralysis. Press and President are said to have engaged in a skillfully contrived collusion to conceal the photographic evidence of his infirmity. A "careful strategy" of concealment and disguise removed this political liability. "Roosevelt dominated his times from a wheel chair, yet he was simply not perceived as being in any major sense disabled." [24]

This is not so. Contemporary accounts of Roosevelt's life, particularly those published in the early years of his presidency, dwell heavily on his paralysis. The sudden illness, long recuperation, and return to politics present a familiar sequence in Roosevelt biographies, embellished with anecdotes of Warm Springs and the generous fortitude of Eleanor Roosevelt. These works were not limited to the elite. Newspaper articles and political pamphlets—both those supporting and those opposing him—deal with Roosevelt's illness and consequent paralysis. [25] Even the *Picture Story of Franklin D. Roosevelt,* a book intended "for very young children," details the President's handicap. [26] Nor were illiterates immune: "literally millions of people saw him moving down his railway ramp, bent over like a praying mantis, or hobbling painfully slowly on the arm of his son." [27]

Roosevelt's exits and entrances were prolonged and clumsy, despite the most careful choreography. As James MacGregor Burns notes, "speaking in halls was difficult; sometimes the candidate had to be carried up fire escapes and backstairs." [28] Each entrance and exit multiplied the number who were forced to recognize Roosevelt as a cripple. People watched these passages "as though hypnotized," and they remembered them.[29]

Roosevelt's return to politics was marked by his appearance at the Democratic National Convention of 1924. Before he spoke, his infirmity had marked him out. Special seating had been provided for him. He arrived early and left late, but even so "the galleries were often still filled and Roosevelt would be recognized and applauded as he struggled down the aisle."[30] This was the scene of Roosevelt's "Happy Warrior" speech nominating Al Smith. The success of this speech in reestablishing Roosevelt as a political actor has been much remarked. What is less noticed, now, though, it was much noticed then, is that Roosevelt's vigorous, vital, and enthusiastic speech was bracketed between unavoidable revelations of an extensive and evidently permanent handicap. Roosevelt's walk to the podium "took a long time. He would place the left crutch forward, shifting his weight over onto his left leg, freeing his right leg and hitching it forward, and then move his right crutch up, shifting his weight back on his right leg, and hitching his left leg forward . . . it was an arduous business."[31] When Roosevelt reached the podium, he paused and, in a characteristic gesture, smiled exuberantly. "The audience went wild. Applause and then cheers filled the Garden. It was an electric moment remembered for many years by all who were present." At the end of the speech, Roosevelt was helped to his chair and wheeled from the hall.

Roosevelt's determined effort to push himself to the limits of his handicap did not enable him to deny or disguise it. It marked him out. It fascinated observers. One watcher could recall, thirty years later, the effect of one of Roosevelt's exits.

The distance from desk to street could not have been more than a hundred feet, but it took the Governor an amazingly long time to traverse it. . . . The audience, as though hypnotized, did not leave. It stood and watched the Roosevelts depart. . . . Finally the Roosevelts reached the street. The audience, still hypnotized, followed them outside.

When their car finally pulled away, he recalled, "An audience of strangers had become a group of friends."[32] There is an element of sadistic voyeurism in those who watched (and in me as I recall) Roosevelt's display of his deformity. Nietzsche observes that cruelty is festive. In the observation of another's affliction, we celebrate our own exemption from this particular pain, this particular deformity. Yet this celebration of exemption contains, in its recognition of the other's pain, the acknowledgment of a common vulnerability. We know the other suffers because we know the other has a form like our own, subject to the same needs, having the same sensations. The recognition of Roosevelt's distinctive affliction brought with it recognition of his representative character. This was enhanced by the political significance of his paralysis.

During his campaigns, Roosevelt would have to be carried over, up, and through entrances not designed for access by the handicapped. Frances Perkins recalled, "He came up over that perilous, uncomfortable, and humiliating 'entrance' and his manner was pleasant, courteous, enthusiastic." Roosevelt was manifestly maimed by the disease; he was paralyzed, crippled, weak, forced to rely on the strength of others, unable to stand, as Americans say, "on his own two feet." These are not the attributes of a leader, least of all in America, where physical prowess has figured prominently in the mythology of leadership.[33] But in America in the midst of the Great Depression, they were the attributes of a representative. "Economic paralysis lay all about." "Paralysis . . . had gripped them."[34] "The thought that America, a nation crippled by the Great Depression, would choose a crippled President to lead it back to prosperity was unthinkable."[35] With denial or disguise impossible, as accounts indicate it was, that is exactly what Americans did.

Faith, especially faith in abstractions, in signs and in signification, had collapsed in the depression. When Hoover sought to revive that faith, to reassure the nation, in speech, of economic recovery, he was not believed. When Roosevelt assured them, "We have nothing to fear but fear itself," he was believed. This was not, as many have argued, merely because he was not Hoover. The depression may have ensured Hoover's defeat, but it did not ensure the triumph of his successor. The collapse of faith in signs necessitated a return to nonarbitrary signification; it demanded a congruence between the signifier and the signified. Roosevelt offered this.

The nation was in a state of economic paralysis, crippled by natural disasters. Roosevelt was also paralyzed, crippled by an act of nature. There was thus an overt material identity between Roosevelt and the nation. He could be recognized as representative without recourse to that faith in abstractions that the collapse of central economic significations had undermined. The multiple referents Roosevelt entailed as signifier played a crucial role in determining the meaning of his presidency. The nation was economically paralyzed. Roosevelt was paralyzed. But Roosevelt came from a family of great wealth, power, and prestige. He possessed these himself. This apparent contradiction in Roosevelt as signifier enabled him to simultaneously represent and subvert the image of the nation as paralyzed and impotent. It was thus not an excess of tact but the recognition of this significant contradiction that led cartoonists to emphasize Roosevelt's legs.

Individuals in the depression found themselves unable to stand on their own two feet. They were forced to rely on the strength of others. Robert MacElvaine's collection of letters from the "down and out" to public officials and public agencies reveals with particular clarity the humiliation, shame, and inadequacy felt by those who needed aid.[36] Those who saw Roosevelt realized, with Frances Perkins, "that this man had accepted the ultimate humility that comes from being helped physically." And he had retained his dignity. Roosevelt's infirmity did make it possible, in Perkins's words, "for the common people to trust him to understand what it is to be handicapped by poverty and ignorance as well as by physical misfortune."[37] It was, however, more profoundly significant. Roosevelt's physical hardship represented their own. He accepted the aid his condition made necessary, and he was undiminished. He enabled them to accept the aid his administration would offer without humiliation. It is not surprising then that innumerable requests for aid were sent not to the agencies, even when their names were known, but to Roosevelt personally.[38] Roosevelt performed a final, and decisive, signification for individuals. He was, like the nation and people he signified, crippled. Yet he was the President, the possessor of enormous power. He thus represented their condition to them as insignificant, asserting once again the primacy of subjectivity, the power of will over objective reality.

This assertion was made more profound by the source of

Roosevelt's authority. Roosevelt had derived his power from his paralysis. Will Durant, reporting on Roosevelt's convention speech for the *New York World* describes him as "beyond comparison the finest man that has appeared at either convention. . . . A figure tall and proud even in suffering; a face of classic profile, pale with years of struggle against paralysis . . . a man softened and cleansed and illumined by pain." [39] Roosevelt's paralysis had made him representative and granted him authority. It had won him allies and, Frances Perkins believed, resolved old enmities. It would also increase his personal authority by likening him to mythic heroes in general and, in particular, to the most significant exemplar of leadership in the American mythology. Alfred Jones writes, "Roosevelt's battle with poliomyelitis during the Twenties not only demonstrated his courage and determination, but also constituted, in a sense, his rite of passage." [40] Roosevelt's reemergence into political life at the 1924 convention was a resurrection. He had, as mythic figures often do, a period of isolation and impotence. It was marked, as mythic ordeals often are, by suffering. The suffering had transformed him in the eyes of the press and the public. It would make him representative of the nation. In 1924 it set him apart. Some understood the paralysis and the national recovery as stigmata and miracles. "Who is this man?" a woman asked a child. "Why, who else but Saint Roosevelt!" the child responded. The woman agreed, "indeed we all feel if there ever was a Saint. He is one." Another wrote Mrs. Roosevelt that looking at his picture "seems to me like looking at the picture of a Saint." To others, "it seems as though some Moses had come." [41]

The 1930s saw an efflorescence of Lincoln scholarship and, more importantly, of Lincoln myth. Suffering was a central trait of the mythic Lincoln. He was "the martyr President." Vachel Lindsay writes,

> He cannot sleep
> . . . .
> His head is bowed
> . . . .
> He carries on his shawl wrapped shoulders now
> The bitterness, the folly and the pain. [42]

Photographic essays document his transformation by suffering. This trait might not have been sufficient to liken Roosevelt to Lincoln, but there were more. Like Lincoln, Roosevelt presided over a time of trials. Letters to Hoover, full of condemnation, call out for "a few Statesmen, oh for just one Statesmen, as fearless as Abraham Lincoln, the emancipator who died for us." People "hoped and trusted that Mr. Roosevelt would be another Lincoln." It was Lincoln's persona that was bestowed on Roosevelt with his election. The success of economic policies further likened him to Lincoln by making him a latter-day "Savior." [43] Fiorello La Guardia, speaking on Lincoln's birthday, declared that "seventy five years from today our present President, Franklin Delano Roosevelt, will be hailed as a liberator, just as we are hailing Lincoln." [44] This was particularly true for blacks who deserted the Republican party in droves. Nancy Weiss, writing on this abrupt transformation of black voting patterns, observes,

> No matter what his racial intent, Lincoln was the father of emancipation, no matter what *his* racial biases, Roosevelt was the father of the New Deal. That made him the second emancipator, the inheritor of Lincoln's mantle, "the best friend the Negro American has had in the White House since Abraham Lincoln," "the Modern Abe Lincoln of the race." [45]

The association of Roosevelt with blacks and emancipation was enhanced by Eleanor Roosevelt's evident sympathy with the emerging civil rights movement. The cultural assumption that a wife's acts and sympathies were subject to the approval and encompassed within the responsibilities of her husband, enhanced Franklin Roosevelt's resemblance to Lincoln, for whites as well as blacks. "How much of a Lincoln does Roosevelt have in him?" Max Lerner asked, "More, I am convinced, than any President since Lincoln or before." [46]

Alfred Jones describes in some detail the efforts made by Roosevelt's advisors—and by Roosevelt himself—to liken him to Lincoln. They were aided in this enterprise by the Lincoln literati: Carl Sandburg, Stephen Vincent Benét, and Robert Sherwood. Benét, in an election day poem, writes that Roosevelt "knows the tides and ways of the People as Abe Lincoln knew the wind on the prairies." [47] He was, Sandburg writes, "the best light of democracy that has occupied the White House since Lincoln." [48] Sherwood writes Roosevelt, "I wish with all my heart to offer my services, for whatever they're worth, to you in this crucial year and to the cause which is yours as surely as it was Lincoln's." [49] Roosevelt himself appealed increasingly to Lincoln as a legitimating paradigm for his conduct in office. On the campaign trail he quoted Lincoln against the Liberty League, to college students opposing America's entrance into the war, and, devastatingly, against Republicans, who found themselves unable to reclaim the image—and the imprimatur—of their founder. In 1939 he had asked, "Does anyone maintain that the Republican Party from 1864 to 1938 was the party of Lincoln?" and characterized that claim as "absurd." In 1940 he severed Lincoln from the signification of party. "I do not know which party Lincoln would belong to if he were alive in 1940—and I am not even concerned to speculate on it . . . his sympathies and motives of the championship of humanity itself have made him for all centuries to come the legitimate property of all parties—of every man and woman and child in every part of our land." [50]

Lincoln's posthumously validated charisma had transformed him from partisan President to national martyr. Roosevelt's ordeal, his role as "Emancipator" and "Savior of the Union," his association with blacks, and his role as war President likened him to Lincoln. He cultivated that likeness. It enabled him to lay claim to more than presidential authority. Lincoln's institutional legacy to Roosevelt was a broad interpretation of the war powers. As heir to Lincoln's mythic persona, Roosevelt was able to transform himself, as events had transformed Lincoln, from a partisan President to national leader. In doing so, he transformed his enemies. Partisan opponents, contesting policy, became, in Roosevelt's words, "Vallandighams." Their dissidence became disloyalty, for they now opposed not a party but the nation. The recovery had already transformed Roosevelt, in the eyes of many, from politician to "saint." He was in Lincoln's place. He signified, the authoritative Sandburg argues, what Lincoln signified: the common people, the rights of labor, universal democracy, the salvation of the union.[51] Roosevelt's accordance to Lincoln's paradigm for charismatic leadership enabled him to extend his authority beyond the limits drawn by law and custom.

Reagan, Roosevelt, and Revision

The history of Roosevelt's authority presents a curious counterpoint to Lincoln's. Where Lincoln's authority increased dramatically upon his death and steadily thereafter, Roosevelt's has waned. Lincoln underwent an apotheosis; Roosevelt declined from saint to consummate politician, from a man above partisanship and governmental constraints to the sign of a constraining government. Reagan's reading of Roosevelt offers an epilogue to Roosevelt's brief mythic ascendancy, and evidence that Roosevelt's paralysis remains significant.

Reagan's autobiography *Where's the Rest of Me?* details at least two transformations: from actor to politician, from "Roosevelt liberal" to Republican conservative. In Reagan's life, as he reads it there, the question "Where's the rest of me?" heralded the end of his acting career and foreshadowed his career as politician. This was his finest line in his finest role—until politics. He employs it to signify his realization that acting was not enough. His political activities presented the answer, supplying that "rest of him" that Reagan felt was missing. During his career as an actor Reagan had identified politically with Roosevelt and the Democratic party. In the performance he considered the apex of his career he played a role that obliged him to identify himself with Roosevelt in a subjective, and profoundly significant, manner. Reagan played a man who had lost his legs, as Roosevelt had lost the use of his, and who, like Roosevelt, overcame that handicap to acquire power and prestige. Reagan mentions the character's triumph over the handicap only in passing, but he dwells at length on the subjective experience of finding himself without legs.

Reagan presents this role as signifying the incompleteness of his life as an actor. The association of the role with Roosevelt, Reagan's positioning of this episode in the narrative, and Reagan's characterizations of his early political identification, indicate that his incompleteness applied to his political opinions as well. Identification with Roosevelt was identification with a cripple, with impotence.

Reagan describes himself in this period as a "hemophiliac liberal." His father, who represents the Democratic party in Reagan's narrative, is, as a WPA administrator, closely associated with the memory of Roosevelt and the New Deal. He is introduced on the first page of Reagan's autobiography, his weakness contrasted with Reagan's infant vitality. Throughout Reagan's narrative his father is identified with weakness, dependence, and democracy. Each account of Jack Reagan's Democratic principles—his concern for equality, for the poor—is coupled with a display of his father's weakness. The Democratic party became, in Reagan's reading, the party of the crippled, the weak, the diseased, and the defective. Reagan's discovery of the rest of him became not merely involvement in politics but involvement in a politics of strength, in which the runners carrying the torch of the 1984 Olympics could figure in a film extolling the strong America of Reagan's administration.[52] The identification of the Democratic party with weakness, the Republican party with strength, was perhaps the greatest of Reagan's rhetorical successes. These amended signs mark Reagan's deft, perhaps unconscious, but nevertheless thoroughgoing, reconstruction of American political discourse. Reagan constructed his persona from the heroic mythology of the Western frontier. His use of that mythology, and its derivatives, as a source of metaphors for contemporary politics changed the dominant referential context of American political discourse. This change in primary referents changed the meaning of Roosevelt and of the signs and gestures commonly employed by the Democratic Party. Western use of physical strength as the signifier of ideal strength enabled Reagan to alter the significance of the Democratic party reformed by—and after—Roosevelt. The inclusion of the poor, of blacks, of women, and of the handicapped had once served as gestures signifying the party's representation of the nation by signifying its representation of those liminal groups on its farthest borders. In this altered context, these gestures became signs of a fundamental weakness.

The question Reagan asked of himself, "Where is the rest

111

of me?" is asked, again and again, of history. It will be answered, again and again, in subsequent revaluations. Presidents assume authority, over themselves and their predecessors, in the creation of their literary selves, but they are made subject to the authority in their turn. Reagan's literary self, like Roosevelt's, will be amended, elaborated, and revalued as consecutive presents look to their pasts.

Authority and Ambivalence

The ambivalences of presidential authority are not confined to control over the content of the Presidents' literary selves. The institutional structures that govern presidential politics are marked by ambivalence as well.

The aggrandizement of presidential power, as Jeffrey Tulis observes, owes much to increasing presidential use of the strategic rhetorical position of the office.[53] This strategic position may have been enhanced by technological advances—most notably the immediate national access afforded by radio and television—but it lies in the very structure of the office.

Two of the virtues of monarchy, in Hegel's view, are its singularity and its embodiment. These two qualities enable the monarch to give material expression to will, to subjectivity. The singularity of the presidency, the ceremonial functions the President performs as head of state, and his role as commander in chief all designate the President as either the momentary representative of the nation as a whole or the permanent commander of some part that acts on behalf of the whole. Thus the performance of his constitutionally designated functions continually constructs him as representative of the nation, though this role is not explicitly assigned to him constitutionally.

This construction was fortified not only by technological advances but also by institutional and ideological changes (the expansion of the military, and of the civilian bureaucracy, increased American involvement in foreign affairs, the triumph of nationalism over states' rights) that increased the effective power of the presidency. These changes were themselves preceded, prompted, and legitimated by the conception of executive power historically inscribed on monarchy. *Executive* and *head of state* entailed references to these extant traditions that could not be wholly suppressed. They were, however, radically altered. The President was recognized as deriving power directly from what Madison called "the fount of all authority," the people.

This dimension of the presidency gives access, as Tulis recognizes, to rhetorical strategies involving direct, and informal, appeals to the people. These have given the President access to an authority over history that extends beyond the constitutional confines of the office.   113

The acquisition of this authority depends, however, on an ironic preliminary. The candidate must be elected. In the process of running for office the candidate is as discreetly divested of authority as the president will later be invested with it. The authority we take for granted in the presidency is here put into question.

The Candidate as Commodity

Candidates appear on television in two ways: on the news and in ads. In each, they find authority difficult to obtain. In each they figure not as authors but as texts, not as productive but as commodities.

The candidates who appear on the news are constructed not only by themselves but by the cameramen, producers, editors, and newscasters who prepare and present reports of campaign appearances. They choose which portions of the candidates' speech or press conference or casual remarks to air. They select the images that will accompany the reports. The candidates' appearances becomes their texts to edit.

Candidates and their staffs have responded to this in a manner that reduces their authority, while appearing to increase it. They have taken the concerns of the media for their own, adopting their preference for appropriately sized sound bites and compelling images. This may, on some occasions, when their predictions are correct and their taste accords with that of the editors, enable them to influence—perhaps even to determine—the content of the news. This is no victory.

The greatest danger to candidates lies not in the content but in the form of the news. Those who have grown up with television, even with radio, know that legions of editors and ranks of machines stand between them and the candidate. They know that what they hear was chosen for them. They think it likely (and they are correct) that what they hear was written by one member of the staff and chosen by another, recorded (in an abbreviated form), edited, and attached to similarly edited images by a television team. They know that much is lost in this sieve of production. They know that what emerges is the product not of the candidate but of a system of production in which the candidate figures not as author but as a resource.

114

Television, at first glance, appears to offer access, overcoming time and space, to candidates on the campaign trail. Television appears to offer the candidate a wider audience; it appears to offer the viewer a chance to see the candidate "up close, and personal." No one speaks directly to the people on the news. Between the electorate and the candidate many have intervened. There are those who present the news, those who edit it, those who decided what to tape, and those who taped it. There are those who decide how much time to give to the campaign on a given day, and those who decide the space that campaigns should occupy in the news. Behind these there are others. There are those who decided what the candidate should say, how it should be said, and when to say it. Behind these there are those who selected the candidate in the primary, those who selected the candidates for it, and those who decided how the selection should be conducted. Most of those who watch know they have had little part in this. They may come to suspect that the candidate has little more.

Recent attention to the use of the media has only enhanced this popular perception. The recognition of the power of form and representation by candidates has led to the proliferation of "handlers," "spin-doctors," and other media consultants. These appear, to a people conscious of the authority of form, as the powers behind the throne, as technological Richelieux.

The terms *handler* and *spin doctor* confirm this impression. The first implies that the candidate is, like an unruly animal, less intelligent than the handlers and requires discipline and restraint. The term *spin doctor* is still more interesting, for in it the candidate is almost completely erased. The candidate figures here only as the source of an ungoverned, undirected energy. The acts, speeches, appearances, and offhand statements of contending candidates are merely raw material, a force to be controlled and directed by experts.

Those whose fortunes are dependent on their ability to predict, chronicle, and analyze public opinion also exercise authority over the candidate. The interpretations and predictions offered on newscasts and in the polls are highly influential. They supersede personal analysis, first by the speed with which they arrive, and secondly because they designate to a national audience those elements in the network of meaning that constitute the political culture to which the speech or gesture refers. Individuals, singly and collectively, are told what they think of a candidate or a candidate's statement before they have had time to think it. They are confronted, directly (in the form of a survey) or indirectly (through the media's coverage of such polls and analyses), with a set of responses to the candidate, and obliged to choose which of these thoughts they think. All other responses are precluded or rendered insignificant. Later discussion, though it may move away from these initial interpretations, is nevertheless predicated upon them, responsive to them, and oriented in relation to the categories they established.

By precluding, or displacing, discordant individual and subcultural interpretations of the speech or gesture's frame of reference, these designations in the media, and later in the academy, enhance the cohesion of the national culture and affective nationality. They reinforce the dominant culture, diminish or disguise the influence of subcultures, and encourage the alienation of minorities and the dissident or disaffected. In this interpretive economy, the most successful rhetorical appeals are likely to be those derived from the dominant culture, readily identified, and nationally accessible. In this process, the majoritarian influence over thought that Tocqueville feared is rendered routine.

The candidate, many items removed from the watching electorate, has two roles in this process of production: resource and product. The candidates' effects, and the outcome of the election, are seen not as the work of the candidates themselves but of those who handle them. The election is no longer seen as a contest between contending candidates but as a complex struggle between opposed sets of handlers and spin doctors, and the media, all of whom engage in a struggle to determine the outcome by determining the meaning of the campaign.

The presentation of the candidate as a product in the production of news is reiterated in the candidate's political advertising. Consider the classic form of the political ad. Political advertisements commonly focus on the candidate, engaged in some activity perhaps, or interspersed (if the producers have pretensions to sophistication) with shots of some evocative setting. The candidate appears not as author of the text but as a part of it, written, like the rest, by the unseen authorities who fashion the form, and control the content, of the commercial. But the candidate who appears in an ad appears not simply as product but as commodity. The content of political advertisements may differentiate them from ads for beer or cereal, but the form remains to mark them as the same. In producing political advertising, candidates, their staffs, and their consultants have adopted the conventions of commerce. Candidates, bound by the commercial form, are obliged to present themselves as commodities. No candidate can do this without surrendering authority; no citizen can watch it without some cynicism. We all know what ads are for. Ads sell things. They sell, most often, things you would not otherwise wish to buy, at prices you would not otherwise be willing to pay. They manufacture needs. They are compounded of (if not outright lies) subtle deceptions and exaggerations. The candidates have to sell themselves. We are asked to buy the line they are selling.

The construction of candidates as commodities conveys a message that one can scarcely fail to note. Each political ad we see informs us that politicians are for sale. One might argue, with some justice, that Watergate, Wedtech, and HUD persuaded us of the corruption of politicians far more effectively than the forms of campaign advertising. Scandals, however, retain their particularity. Watergate, though it may have tarnished our view of politicians as a species, hurt the Republicans more than the Democrats, and Nixon more than Ford. The corruption at HUD revealed the criminal rapacity of particular individuals, and a particular administration. Like rain falling alike on the just and the unjust, the forms of political advertising incriminate the most scrupulous of candidates. They imbed even an unquestioned, perhaps unquestionable, integrity in a form that silently and insistently mocks and impugns it.

Attention to the meaning attached by the conventions of advertising to the persons of the candidates reveals the presence of particular impediments to the candidacies of blacks and women. A white man who is for sale is corrupt; a black man for sale is a slave. A white man who "sells himself" is success- **117** ful; a woman who "sells herself" is a prostitute. The language—and the forms—of commerce are neither race- nor gender-neutral. The proposal of Senators Daniel Inouye, Wendell Ford, and Warren Rudman that political ads have a common format, presenting only the candidate, presumed the neutrality of a form that is far from neutral. The construction of candidates as commodities, though it does no good service to white men, weighs far more heavily on women and on blacks.

The alternative proposal of Senators Ernest Hollings and John Danforth showed a far-more-sophisticated understanding of the texts of television. The senators, troubled by the prevalence of "negative advertising," proposed that candidates be required to appear and speak in any ads that mentioned their opponents. As Michael Oreskes aptly puts it in the *New York Times,* "Whoever wanted to slash an opponent would have to stand there with the knife." [54] As Oreskes also notes, the proposal was received with predictable outrage from those who believed that in regulating content it would restrict freedom of speech. They were misled.

The Hollings-Danforth proposal did not dictate to these authors what they might or might not say; it merely asked them to sign their work. The proposal recognized that videotape is text, that visual images convey political messages, and that the careful construction of the image may divorce the candidate from that text. The Hollings-Danforth proposal demanded a degree of responsibility from candidates and offered them the opportunity to recoup a portion of their lost authority, constructing them not as products or commodities but as the authors of these political texts.

Efforts to improve campaign advertising have focused, almost without exception, on the content rather than the form of the ads. Newscasters, reporters, and commentators regularly remark on the level or vitriol in a given campaign, and legislators, as we have seen, attempt to limit it. Their condemnations present "negative campaigning" as a novelty and a development whose undesirability is manifest. Anyone even slightly familiar with the history of American politics scoffs at the notion that negative campaigns are novel. When Molly Ivins writes of Reagan that if his IQ sank any lower we'd have to water him twice a day, she is perpetuating a tradition of invective that reaches well beyond the founding of the Republic. Like other legacies of the early Republic, however, this too has fallen into disuse.

Denunciations of "negative campaigning" may have effects far more dispiriting than the modes of discourse they condemn. They accord very badly with the often attendant contention that contemporary campaigns lack substance, passion, and attention to the issues. The convention that one ought not to call one's opponent a liar, a thief, a thug, a warmonger, a murderer of unborn children, or a half-deaf geriatric with the intellect of a cauliflower may be well suited to the dinner table, but it is not suited to the campaign trail or the Congress. It may be good manners, but it is not good politics. Those who believe each fetus is a child speak the truth as they know it when they accuse their opponents of murder. When someone shows an unseemly willingness to spill the blood of young men and women in an ill-defined cause, it is not too harsh to call such a person a warmonger. Invective may be impolite; it may be inflammatory. It need not, however, be untrue. Though invective may be uncivil, it serves civil ends. It indicates to those who watch and listen that the issues concerned are issues of moment, gravity, and urgency, where passion is appropriate and moderation irrational.

The campaign for "positive" advertising has largely displaced the campaign for truth in advertising because all advertising carries with it an aura of falsity, of misrepresentation. Several advertisements in the 1980s turned on this assumption. The best known are the "Joe Isuzu" advertisements in which a man with an ostentatiously shifty manner makes all sorts of ostentatiously incredible claims for the Isuzu. The ads satirize the characteristic content of car advertisements, a byword for deception in popular culture. Their mocking stance aligned the absent, but implicit, Isuzu dealers with the mocking and suspicious audience, against competing dealers.

Advertising is another instance of supplementarity in popular culture. Marketing presents itself as something that is done with the product rather than to it. Advertisements are presented as additions rather than alterations. Yet once one recognizes that commodities function as signs, as elements of a language, one recognizes that advertising does more than market the product; it (re)produces it. Investing the product with additional layers of meaning, traits, and associations alters the product's constitution. The advertised product replaces the product it purports to represent.

119

Neither candidates nor commentators can afford to adhere to the notion that campaign commercials are supplementary strategies in the simple sense. The electorate, consciously or not, has long abandoned it. People elected to have not only Reagan in the presidency but "morning in America."

Television has served thus far as a place for candidates or parties to sell themselves. We might think of it instead as a way to say what cannot so easily be said in words. The virtue of the image is its capacity for evocative economy and its reach. The former quality, if it is to be exploited democratically, liberally, must assimilate the image to the word, making televised images as well as televised texts objects of debate, reflection, and contention.

Sight and Power

The American regime, which placed its founding under the gaze of a watching world, still subjects itself to the gaze of a watchful people. The reach of television into neighborhoods and homes makes it a commonplace. The use of television to place government under the gaze of the governed makes contemporary practice an expression of historic principles. Through the television citizens take on the surveillance of their government; they act as guardians. The popular capacity for surveillance of the government, though it is augmented by the press and television, remains limited. The perception of surveillance is, however, stronger and more effective than these limitations would seem to warrant.

Those who watched the Watergate hearings saw those who held power brought unwillingly into the public eye. They saw them subjected to the gaze, their actions, their words, their secrets revealed. All who watched participated directly in this exercise of the power of surveillance, a power they held collectively. Those who watched knew that they watched with their compatriots. They knew that their watching was a sign and an exercise of a power held (as it was then exercised) collectively. The President, the President's men, and the congressional committee came under the watching eye of the people.[55]

The televised Watergate hearings were not, however, simply an employment of the people's power of surveillance. They inverted a complex visual economy intimately connected to Nixon's exercise of power. More than most Presidents, Nixon was conscious of the relation of sight to power. He had won a notable victory through self-display in the Checkers speech. He had been defeated, so it was said, by Kennedy's superior command of appearances in the televised debates of 1960. Great matters and small details of his presidency reveal the importance of the visual economy to the office. There was the spectacular visit to China, preceded by a series of secret trips and covert negotiations, and there was the spectacular failure of Nixon's attempt to alter the appearance of the White House guards. The hearings inverted the established visual economy. The President was no longer on display; he was under surveillance. He could command the gaze, but he could also be commanded to subject himself to it. He had held covert meetings, kept secrets. Those meetings, and those secrets, were revealed. The end was multiply ironic. Nixon's attempt to extend his surveillance over the Democratic party, and then to conceal this attempt, were the occasion for his undoing. The means that he had employed to keep his subordinates under his surveillance became the means for making his secrets public.[56]

Sight is power in several senses. There is the power of surveillance, and there is power in display. The capacity for surveillance is an instrument of power. The capacity to make oneself visible, to be seen, is a prerogative, and hence a sign, of power. To be prominent is to be powerful. Obscurity is a mark of impotence. The conventions that made the king's display of his person a display of his power did not evaporate with the decline of monarchy. Convention gives the President the capacity to command coverage of his speeches and press conferences.[57] No other officials are conceded this ability to put themselves on public display at will.

The importance of the visual economy to the presidency is intimately related to the President's role as sign. The singularity that enables the President, like Hegel's monarch, to embody individuality, subjectivity, and national unity in a manner plurality denies the legislature depends on sight. The embodiment of the presidency enables the President to present an image of the people to itself: singular, united, with a common material form and a single will. The legislature presents an image of the people in itself: divided, comprising a great diversity, debating, doubting, driving, sometimes finding expression in common judgments and a common will.

In politics, as in philosophy, the desire for wholeness has proved not only errant but divisive.

FOUR

Our Homeland the Text

THE CONSTITUTION IS AT ONCE text and nation. It is the act that founds the nation and the sign that marks it. It is the expression and annunciation of collective identity, at once the people's advent and their epiphany. It is an effort to represent what the people are and to record what they have been. It reconstructs, as all such representations do, the present and the past that it records. It reveals, as all such representations do, that those who represent remake themselves.

The act of writing a nation's Constitution—of constituting a nation in writing—is not only (as the preceding ambivalent litany suggests) an act replete with contradictions but also an act of reflection ending in a singular clarity of vision. In the act of constituting themselves in writing, the people recognize their authority. They become conscious of their power. They recognize—that is, they rethink and reconsider—the meaning, character, and origin of their authority. They know themselves as author.

The American Constitution begins with the assumption by the people of their own authority. The recognition is marked twice in this text, once in the content and once in the form of the words. The annunciation of authority is made in words written before the rest, in a larger, bolder hand. The shape of the letters, the form of the text as well as its content, invests the assumption of authority with particular importance. The use of writing to mark these words, this sign, out from the rest inscribes upon the text as signifier a recognition of the importance of writing itself. In this use of the material rather than the ideal qualities of writing, the people inscribe upon the text, and hence in their own nationality, an acknowledgment of the importance of writing to their constitution. They do more in writing their constitution than inscribing their nationality. They include in this inscription a sign that they do so mindfully, in full recognition of the power of inscription to transform identity.

The act of constitution, written or no, is an act of transubstantiation. In it we see not the word made flesh but the flesh made word. Many bodies find themselves in a name—*America* or *la Republique*. They exchange their material constitution for an ideal constitution of their own devising.

This self-engendered transubstantiation enables the people, as citizens, as sovereign, and, most importantly, as author, to transcend the limits of their existence in the flesh. As the members of an ideal body, a *corpus mysticum*, they survive the deaths of their various corporeal bodies. As the author of the national constitution, they can speak, and they can dictate, even when their bodies are silent in death. The transubstantiation thus invests them with more than the capacity for survival beyond the natural, physical limits of their species. In this transubstantiation they acquire the capacity for temporal imperialism. Their naming, like that of the god of Genesis, is an act of creation. It calls into being a new world order. Their posterity will be born into this order, governed by the structures and mindful of the ends that it establishes. Theirs is the dead hand of the past that may weigh so heavily (or give so much assistance) to the living. They become the conquerors of history.

Temporal imperialism is, however, an undertaking as ambiguous as its territorial counterpart. The conquerors will be remade by their conquest, constituted not only now as founders but as authors of regimes and peoples they never knew. Those whose constitutions they authored take their name. As this phrase implies, this act of acquiescence and subjection is also an act of appropriation and authority. The character and actions—the constitution—of the conquered will determine the meaning and significance of the founding. As the nation endures, the founders will find themselves in different histories, with different aspects of their lives and project differently understood. As figures of history and public myth they will become the creations of their posterity. The founders become not only the conquerors but the conquered of history. This is the surest sign of their success. **125**

The transubstantiation that makes of these assembled bodies one people, one ideal nation, gives them one name. In this name they transcend their differences and multiplicity. They make one out of many. In authoring this new, ideal being, they overcome the isolation and incompletion of their corporeal individuality.

The most profound articulations of the consequences of this entrance into an identity in language are to be found in Rousseau and Lacan. Rousseau describes the transformation effected by the social contract as a transformation not simply of condition but of kind. It invests men with faculties they did not possess in nature, among them, intelligence, morality, sexuality, property.[1] Lacan, likewise convinced of the alteration effected in one's constitution by the entry into collective life, sees in this (as Plato, Hegel, and Freud had before him) a splitting of one from another, of one from oneself.[2] The acquisition of authority, of the capacity to inscribe oneself on the external world, comes at the price of one's singularity and makes one subject to the words themselves.[3]

Lacan's elegant and profound account of the grandeur and tragedy of man's transubstantiation obliges us to recognize that the act of constituting a political identity is not simply the victory of mind over matter, the triumph of the will in the world. It supplements a corporeal with a written constitution. The citizens of an inscribed nation, the authors of written constitutions, take upon themselves a written identity. Those who are constituted in politics and language give their ideal and political constitution primacy over their natural constitution. In the same way, those who write their constitutions come to regard "written" as "real" identities.

This privileging of the written over other forms shows itself quite markedly in American political culture, indeed, in all the written, constitutionalist cultures of the West. In such nations, without writing there is no identity. The people know themselves to be constituted in language. They know their homeland is the text.[4]

126

The transubstantiation of word to flesh does not displace the flesh whose satisfactions people continue to enjoy (indeed, in an enhanced form) and whose travails they continue to suffer (again, in an enhanced form). The pursuit of pleasure in the flesh is accomplished through the word. The most seemingly corporeal pursuits, let us say eating and sex, become literary. The process of eating—of chewing, swallowing, digestion, and its vicissitudes—becomes matter for metaphor. Thus Jeremiah speaks of swallowing the honeyed text, and Nietzsche writes of the German inability to digest. The practice of eating becomes the province of recipes and epicures.

The food one eats is not just food; it is food remade, transformed in accordance with written rules, according, in many cases, to a written recipe or a thoroughly inscribed technological process. The experience of eating becomes a subject for literary reflection. M. F. K. Fisher, Auguste Escoffier, and their like author our understanding of what it means to eat well and to enjoy one's food and how one experiences the dryness of wine or the bitterness of unsweetened chocolate. They transform taste as sensation to taste as sensibility.

Sexuality is similarly altered. This "natural drive," this "instinct" we know only through convention, becomes a matter of writing, a literary act. Sexuality is regulated through scriptures. It becomes the focus (or, in more reticent epochs, the absent center) of the literatures of love and romanticism. Again, the act is reconstructed: the meaning of each orifice and organ scripturally established, instructions given, and experiences catalogued, described, defined. It engenders, begets, disseminates, brings forth a fecund body of seductive metaphors.

As the pleasures of the body are rendered and remade in language, the text itself becomes an agent and a medium of pleasures, an object of desire. Readers whose homeland is the text can be aroused by a book, by a picture. Insensate marks upon a page become currency for absent bodies, unperformed acts. The effective presence of erotica and pornography prove the ascendancy of representation. The capacity of these to act upon the body depends upon the ability of representations to call up in that body responses we call natural, instinctive, and physical. Criticisms of the erotic and the pornographic likewise accept the representation as currency for what it represents. The capacity of pornography to shock depends, like its capacity to give pleasure, on the power of representation.[5]

The capacity of erotica and pornography to give pleasure, and to shock, does not, however, depend on a presumed identity between the representation and that which it represents. Quite the contrary. It is quite possible, as any reader knows, to take pleasure in the description of an event that one would rather not experience in the flesh. Readers recognize that representation alters that which it represents.[6] The novels of Poe, Sheridan Le Fanu, and Stephen King testify to our capacity to exploit the space between the representation and that which is represented. The representation becomes a source of pleasure or pain in its own right, not as that which it represents but in relation to it.

Representation alters not only what we read but what we are. The body itself, the literary locus of acts, sensations, and tastes, becomes an inscribed surface, a written text. The color of the skin, and the shape of the eyes, nose, and mouth, become signifiers of race and ethnicity—in some eras, of class and occupation. Meaning is written into them. They become signs. Gender is similarly constituted. Differences in the shape of bodies, in the number of their organs and orifices, in the presence or absence—and the location—of hair, and in their genes are filled with significance. These are natural differences, but as natural differences they are of no moment. They become carriers of meaning only when they cease to be natural. They acquire political significance only when they are transformed from physical to textual differences.

As Hans Georg Gadamer observes, we are in language; it is in language, through language, that we have our being. But bodies are not equally inscribed. We are all constituted in language; we experience pleasure and pain in the flesh through the medium of the word. We are all constituted as agents by this inscription, yet all bodies are not assigned equal agency.

The woman's body becomes a "figure of speech." The phrase itself indicates the capacity of the woman's body, whether present in the flesh or called up by words or context, to alter the meaning of words. *Figure* refers to signs, especially numerical signs; and ciphers, to calculation. When *figure* refers to a woman, it acquires a different and revealing meaning: it refers to the shape of her body. The invocation of femininity transforms a reference to cipher and calculation to a reference to the eroticized body. This is perhaps the most common linguistic effect of the inscription of femininity on words.

As this discussion suggests, the transformation of a corporeal to a written constitution, from flesh to word, is not the only instance of transubstantiation. This word will become flesh in its turn. The Constitution, each constitution and reconstitution, makes citizens in its own image. The constitution of political meaning extends far beyond the structures of the state, beyond parties, beyond quotidian discussions of political controversies. The citizens' conceptions of their identities, individual as well as collective, are irretrievably altered by the process of constituting themselves as a nation. The constitution extends to the ephemera of their daily lives, altering the manner in which they read and write and speak. The constitution enters into their bones, as we say, or (as Scripture has it) "I will write my law upon their inward parts." The flesh becomes word, and that word becomes flesh.

Nor does the process end here. The act of writing a constitution initiates a dialectic in which individuals, citizens, annunciate their identity and comprehend it in its now external and objective form. They are altered by this knowledge of themselves, by the assimilation of (or, if you prefer, their assimilation to) this Constitution. This amended identity will seek utterance and expression in its turn. The people become increasingly self-conscious, increasingly reflective, increasingly willful.[7] This initiation of an unending dialectic of becoming and overcoming is the greatest virtue of constitutionalism.

As this dialectic indicates, the relation between a people and its constitution is inevitably ambivalent. The people construct the text, the text constructs the people. The text enables the people to speak when they are silent, to be present when they are absent, to be when they are not. There are two ambivalent relations here.

The dialectic of mutual construction that marks politics' in constitutional regimes provides a text, or, rather, two texts, of its own. It comprises two linked commentaries: the commentary on the text that may be read in the people that the text constructs, and the commentary on the people that may be read (though, I would argue, no more easily) in the text that they construct.

The realization of the text in the lives of the people—the establishment of the institutions it describes, the accordance (and evasion) of the procedures it sets forth, the assimilation of its vision of the nation's ends, as well as its design by the people and their posterity—reveals much that was hidden in the text. The unanticipated consequences that follow the text's realization prompt realizations of another sort. They endow the people with a greater capacity to comprehend the significance of their constitution. The establishment, the realization in the material world, of each institution and set of procedures that the Constitution describes gives each a certain independence. The institutions and procedures can be observed apart from the text in which they remain embedded. The text's construction of the people, the nation, and the government is thus its own deconstruction.

The people, too, deconstruct themselves in the construction of the text. The text that they construct in the act of writing their Constitution establishes not only distinct institutions and branches of government but also categories of power, categories distinguishing means from ends, and other more subtle categories. This literary construction of the identity and aspirations of the people not only separates them from themselves, it separates certain aspects of their previously inarticulate identity from one another, annunciates these, and brings them to life. Once realized, they reveal tendencies and characteristics in the constitution of the people that once went hidden or unrealized.

These two deconstructions are, of course, inseparably linked. It might therefore seem more sensible to regard both as realizations of the character of the people, and rather precious to insist upon the text as worthy of separate consideration. This is not so. Every people, with or without a constitution (written or unwritten), deconstructs itself historically and in the material artifacts citizens construct in the course of their common life. Those who constitute themselves in writing constitute themselves deliberately, setting their Constitutions apart from themselves, reflecting upon them, entering into a dialogue with the text that becomes a dialectic of construction and deconstruction, alienation and self-knowledge. They have bound themselves to be people of their word.

Those who regard Constitutions simply as realizations of the characters of the people concerned, dismissing the significance of their textual transubstantiation, must also dismiss the significance of the Constitution as promise. The liberal tradition has identified Constitutions with contracts. Others, mindful of the constitutive character of Scripture, regard constitutions as covenants. Whether one regards them as contracts or covenants, whether they bind the king to the people, the people to the king, or the people, as sovereign, to themselves, each constitutes a promise.[8]

In promising one wills one's own constancy. The people in constituting themselves as a nation manifest their will to be true to themselves. In constituting themselves in writing they will be true to their word. In order to be at once true to themselves and true to their word they must become the authors of their own identity, writing and written. Yet they will not surrender the body; they will not completely separate themselves from the changes inherent in corporeality. Nor can they make themselves entirely like-minded. The constancy they seek is undermined by the means that promise to best ensure it.

The act of writing a constitution is an act of signification. In it the people create a representation of their collective character. The representation—in the case of written constitutions, the text of their nationality—is not subject to the vicissitudes that beset them in the flesh. It seems to secure constancy for their collective identity. Yet as we have seen, they are changed by the act itself. They will be changed again, as the Constitution makes a new sort of citizenry, and again, as these newly constituted citizens become the authors of the Constitution they inherit.

Representation—in politics and semiotics—depends upon acceptance of the principle that a thing can be what it is not. Those who accept representative government permit themselves to be represented, to be cast in another form. They surrender their identity to another. In this act, which began as a search for constancy, they acknowledge the inconstancy of their constitutions. They assert that they can remain themselves only by becoming another.

It is fitting, therefore, that they represent themselves in language. Language, whether written or spoken, depends upon the taking of one thing for another. The title to my car is not a car (it does not take gas or move forward), yet if I sign the title to my car over to you, you will own the car more surely than if you drove it to Milwaukee. **131**

Consider a more-telling (though not a more political) example. Luigi Barzini writes that, in the wake of World War II, the French were faced with an infinitely more difficult task than confronted the Italians. The Italians, as Carlo Sforza told him, "had only to forget a defeat. The French had to invent a victory." [9] For a people with a written constitution such a task is not overwhelmingly difficult. The French have succeeded in persuading themselves that France from 1940 to 1945 comprised not the millions of collaborators and quietists who inhabited the area between the English Channel and the Pyrenees but a community of expatriates and criminals, the forces in England under de Gaulle, and those in France who became the maquisards. The rest were not France; they were Vichy.

It would seem that the French are telling us—and themselves—a lie. In a sense they are. It was that sense that led the French to fear the trial of Klaus Barbie. Yet if the French emerged from that trial, as I believe they did, largely unscathed, it was not because of the restraint of the defense. It is because of that quality of language—of representation—that enables a people to be what they are not. The French, in their account of the war, show themselves to be true to their word. Having constituted themselves in writing they prefer that constitution to their imperfect realization of it. They divorce themselves from those who would not be governed by the word, sentencing them to a literary and historic exile. Though the partisans of Vichy remained within the territorial boundaries of the nation, inhabiting the institutions and offices of government, loyal to the regime that ruled France, they are regarded as traitors and aliens. They are foreign to the idea, and to the words, of France.

These noble lies are not peculiar to the French, nor are they confined to the language of the law. The American Constitution is a tissue of such lies. We say to ourselves that all men are created equal, that any child can grow up to be President, that anyone can succeed in America, that Congress shall make no law abridging freedom of speech. We know that people are born with varying endowments in circumstances that ensure

132

their inequality. We know that men are born to bodies invested with a status greater than that of the bodies of women. We know that our freedom of speech is abridged by laws governing the workplace. We lie, and we know we lie. We know that the nation of which we speak and write with such regard does not exist in the world of our experience. But we begin to overcome ourselves in this duplicity.

In these instances of the ascendancy of the rule of law over the rule of men, one sees the virtue of inconstancy. The constitution the people construct for themselves may be, indeed must be, not a promise of loyalty to a form of life already realized in the material world but rather a promise of fidelity to an ideal nation.[10] In writing a constitution each people knows itself to be in a state not of being but of becoming and overcoming.

Those who constitute themselves in writing too often remain willfully unconscious of the unending dialectic of constitution. They prefer to see the writing of the Constitution as the perfect expression of an ideal identity. Those in America who hold this view of the constitutional enterprise mark the founding of the nation (in the ratification of the Constitution) as the achievement of an ideal state.[11] They attempt to bind themselves and their posterity to the preservation—or, as is generally the case, the resurrection—of this perfectly constituted nation.

Acknowledging the impossibility of accomplishing so reactionary a mission, these Americans implicitly exile themselves from the nation they constitute. Repudiating their present in favor of a past material constitution, they mark the nation as already dead to the world. In their reverence for the founding they refuse to recognize themselves as founders. Convinced of the efficacy of the Constitution, they refuse to acknowledge its effects on their own constitution. Their perfervid acclamations of the Constitution's authority only reveal how partial is their understanding of the word.

It is ironic that those Americans who see the founding as a lost golden age, the founders as a generation of demigods, find nothing greater to ascribe to them than an unsuccessful attempt at collective mummification. The irony is somewhat enhanced by the realization that the error made by these is shared by a party they find particularly noxious. Those who have engaged in the enterprise (more popular formerly than at present) of revealing failings of sense and virtue on the part of the founders, concur in regarding the Constitution as the creation of these men, the product of their time.[12]

Both the myth of decline and the crude debunking that is its inevitable consequence deny the text the capacity to transcend the time of its composition. The error is made the more striking, however, by the Constitution's own protest against it. The text is remarkable for its materially, as well as intellectually, conspicuous construction of the reader as author. Acknowledgment of the Constitution's authority, coupled with recognition of the Constitution's author, must persuade one of the dialectical relation between the people and the text. Consideration of this relation reveals that the dialectic must continue while the text retains its constitutional character. There is no end to it. The process of transubstantiation that the writing of the Constitution inaugurates is not simply one from flesh to word and word to flesh. It reiterates a series of earlier transformations from a collective to an individual condition, from an unconscious to a conscious state. This greater dialectic marks a fundamental difference in human constitution. Rather than a state of being, of uniformity and constancy in the constitution of the species and its individual members, humanity is characterized by a condition of inconstancy, a state not of being but of becoming.

The human species is constituted in difference. Its members know themselves as body and mind. The mind is embodied. They know themselves to be embodied through the sensations and the needs of the body. They live materially—eating, sleeping, seeing—and ideally as the intellectual constructs of themselves and others. They know themselves as individuals and as comprehended in collective categories. They regard the collective, therefore, as at once theirs and as other to themselves. In reflecting on themselves in their singularity, each becomes alienated from the self that serves as the object of reflection. Like the text, man is a lie. He is what he is not.

The dialectical relation between a people and the constitution it gives itself has the same effects that Hegel attributes to a greater dialectic. The dialectic impels consciousness. In the process of authoring—as it was authored by—the people, the constitution apprises people of their ambivalence in their ambivalent relation to the text. The act of constitution makes them conscious of themselves. It is not simply that the act of constitution, by providing the people with an objective representation of themselves, makes them newly conscious of their identity, for the process does not end here. The experience of being continually constituted and constituting makes them conscious of themselves as at once ideal and material, moved by the requirements of their material condition to ideal innovations, and expressing these in material form. More than this, the experience of an ambivalent constitution makes them conscious, willful participants in the dialectic. It is in the act of interpretation that this education in ambivalence reaches its culmination.

The written text, which exists beyond the moment of its composition, speaks to the people and their posterity of their identity and aspirations. It claims to speak to them not as an artifact of the past but as the present law. No text, however transcendent, is unmarked by its time. No text, however abstract, speaks to all circumstances. For all of these reasons there will be disjunctions between what is said to be and what is, between a people and its Constitution.

These disjunctions have been marked as crises of legitimacy.[13] They reveal the authority with which the dead hand of the past governs the living. For Marx, and others, they reveal efforts at constitutional legitimation as mere mystifications— efforts by an entrenched class to render its dominion more palatable by disguising its origin and operations. For others, reformers of all sorts, these moments that reveal a disjunction between what is said to be and what is call for a "rectification of names," for the replacement of words whose referents are altered.[14] In each case, these moments of disjunction are marked as revelations of the text's imperfection, and these imperfections as the source of the people's troubles. This is not so. These imperfections are the source of the people's greatness.

The apprehension of difference in the text of the Constitution and the constitution of the people may make the people newly conscious of themselves, of the text, and of that dialectical and ambivalent relation between the ideal and the material that is the condition of man. It will do so when they find themselves compelled to interpretation, confronting their constitution in this difference between the text and their condition. Difference draws them into dialogue with the text. **135**

The text speaks to those it constitutes, annunciating their identity and ends, instructing them in the means for ordering their common life, dictating the design of their governmental institutions. The text acts as author, creating a people, and a set of material circumstances, in its own image. This act of authority alienates, as all such acts do, the text from its author. The disjunctioh between the constitution and the nation it constitutes creates practical (as well as theoretical) questions for those who wish to be true to their word. They have bound themselves to live according to the constitutional text. They are confronted with circumstances the text does not explicitly anticipate and with contradictions revealed, or introduced, as the text is realized. Obliged to live in the altered world their constitution has (in part) created, they are required to abandon or interpret it. They must find within the text answers to problems it did not address, templates for governing unimagined institutions.

Among the litter of abandoned Constitutions, one finds several texts that have served admirably in this fashion. The American Constitution, with its much-praised two hundred years of service, pales before the age and range acquired by the texts belonging to the Peoples of the Book: the Bible, the Koran, the Talmud, and hadith. Interpretation has enabled these texts to endure.

Interpretation transforms a written text from dictate to dialogue, blurring the Socratic distinction between speaking and writing. Constitutional texts inscribe nations. In the case of the American Constitution, as with the Koran, the text may be said to speak them into being.[15] In their newly constituted characters, from their newly constituted circumstances, altered by the text but nevertheless determined to maintain it, people look to the text for answers to the questions raised by their experience. Through them, in them, the material world questions the constitutive text.

This questioning of the text is an act of no small significance. In it the seemingly silent and subservient text speaks up to its author. In it, the questioning people, affirming the transcendence of the text, deny it unilateral authority. They deny that the extant, explicit text is adequate to their needs. They affirm that there is much that is latent and implicit in the text, and that they may be answered by these hidden meanings, counseled, if not ruled, by this covert constitution. Their act suggests that not one but a number of constitutions are comprehended within the text.

Interpretation of the Constitution is thus an ambivalent communion, coupling the people and the text, the material and the ideal, aspiration and experience. In it the people recognize their ambivalent constitution between word and flesh. In it the people recall their authority.

We continue our constitution in this dialogue with the text, as the construing, constructing reader. The questions that the people put to the text are answered not by the text alone but by the intercourse between text and people.

It is interpretation that is the constitutive activity for those who inherit a Constitution, and from interpretation that they derive their authority. This authority is, as all authority must be, both political and semiotic. In interpretation one acquires power not only over the present and future in the rendering of judgments or the design and workings of bureaucratic institutions but over these and the past in the determination of meaning. In extending the meaning of nationality those who interpret alter the significance of the past: what it was, what was done, what came of it. They become authors of themselves, their past, and their posterity. This gives new referents and new importance to the term *self-made man* and obliges us to reconsider the significance of popular authority.

All people are within language. They are constituted in and by the words they use. They acquire from these a common frame of mind, a common set of categories. Language itself, in its qualities of collectivity and utterance, precipitates people into a political world. It is here that the authority of language reveals its ambivalence. Those who are authored by language acquire in their subjection the capacity to become authors themselves. In language they may become their own authors, and the authors of others, for language is the medium of rule.

What differentiates those with written constitutions in the usual sense (documentary expressions of a national identity) is not that they are constituted in writing but that they know themselves as such and mark it appropriately. The possession of a Constitution apprises a people, generation after generation, that they are constituted in language. It is not, however, sufficient to secure to them the authority that is their proper inheritance.

If they are to become their own authors, and, in that act, the authors of their past and their posterity, they are obliged to make the words their own. Those who inherit rather than compose the words that rule them attain this authority in their accession to the words of their Constitution. This accession, like the word that marks it, is ambivalent. They will realize themselves in acceding to the authority of their Constitution over them. They will endeavor to be true to their word, according to their actions to the Constitution, and determining the limits of the nation by the reach of the words that they would have govern them. Yet this accession is also an accession to authority. If they are to make the words their own, they must apply them to altered conditions and to altered citizens. They must reflect on their constitution in the flesh. They must recognize the authority exercised in the transubstantiation of word to flesh. They must elect to exercise that authority in acts of interpretation and critical reflection.

The advocacy of a collective automachia has particular force for Americans, whom the Constitution calls explicitly to interpretation and authority. Because it is written, in a culture where Scripture has long been regarded as authoritative, at a time when people are increasingly conscious of the determinative effects of the form as well as the content of language, it invites Americans to reflect upon writing as constitutive in the broadest sense. Because it invites its own amendment even as it enjoins allegiance, it invites Americans to reflect upon change as the guarantor of constancy, and upon the relation of change and constancy in the definition of identity. Because it acknowledges the people as author of a text they know to have authored them, it invites them to recognize the dialectical nature of constitution. Because they are written into the text, as much in the name of the thing as in its content, it invites them to confirm that writing in the act and the acknowledgment of interpretation as a constitutional activity. It obliges them to be critical if they would be obedient, to comprehend the text if they are to be comprehended within it. It entails on the people collectively the ancient command "Know thyself."

FIVE

Before the Law

AMERICA WAS CONSTITUTED IN THE SPACE between law and outlawry, between legitimacy and rebellion, between the immediacy of the spoken word and the endurance of the written text. America is a nation where "law is king," yet the Americans are also "a people who think lightly of the laws." This constitutive contradiction marks the law as an axis in the structure of American identity.

As Robert Ferguson observes, "The centrality of law in the birth of the republic is a matter of national lore." [1] American ideology, echoing its country party antecedents, counterposed the rule of law to the rule of men. Obedience was transformed. Once deference to another, it was now part of the practice of self-government, an indication not of inferior rank but of the capacity to command.

Veneration of the law led to veneration of those who had mastered it, to an unprecedented regard for the practice and practitioners of the law. Ferguson details the prestige acquired by lawyers in the early national period, their dominance of American politics, and their influence on American letters. [2] Lawyers in contemporary America retain, indeed they have enhanced, their political dominance. They preserve a presence, albeit less distinguished, in American letters. Yet respect for lawyers has not been universal—in historical or contemporary American popular culture. The producer of *Equal Justice* described a particularly nefarious character as "a very smart lawyer. I had people say, you know, a character who's that despicable, I really believe him as a lawyer." [3]

The proclamation that "in America the law is king" came from Thomas Paine, a rebel in a nation of rebels. Americans stand perpetually before the law—as rebels and authors, subjects and guarantors, the critics and creations of its rule. Before the law, there was the nation. The constitutional text is marked as the work of an already present people. Veneration of the Constitution is accompanied by recognition and regard for the revolution that preceded it, the rebellion out of which it came. The development of law has not displaced the right of the people to alter or amend it. Regard for the rule of law defers to the principle that unjust laws do not command obedience. When John Brown, Thoreau, and Martin Luther King, Jr., called upon the people to disobey the law, they spoke as rebels. Yet they were echoed by the state at Nuremberg. The insistence that the law must itself be judged subjects the law to the questions of the citizens.

Representations of Law

The revolutionary sense of the priority of the people to the law, marked in the text of the Constitution, shows itself in the constitution of popular culture. It has traditionally found expression in a regard for popular rebellion, in the recognition of the legitimacy of riot, in the mythology of the outlaw, in the poetry of Walt Whitman, Vachel Lindsey, Amiri Baraka, and Allen Ginsberg. It is given contemporary expression in the songs of Johnny Cash and Willie Nelson, Bruce Springsteen and Public Enemy.

Public Enemy complains of an intrusive government: "The FBI was tappin' my telephone / I never live alone." The group casts itself with outlaws and revolutionaries: "I'm like Nat," "Like Vecsey or Prosser," "Newton, Cleaver and Seale." Like generations of American poets before, Public Enemy identifies a certain disregard for law with popular power: "Power of the people say." [4] Whitman, preceding the group by over a century, calls Americans "a people who think lightly of the laws" and asks scornfully, "States! Were you looking to be held together by the lawyers?" [5]

Television exhibits the same ambivalence before the law present in American canonical documents, American letters, and the rest of American political culture. An extraordinary amount of American popular culture is devoted to dramas of the law. Television alone has brought the fictional courtroom dramas of *Perry Mason* and *Matlock*, the "genuine" trials of *The People's Court*, and the courtroom and office drama of *L.A. Law*. There have been police shows; *Dragnet, Naked City, Hunter, Starsky and Hutch, Miami Vice, Police Woman, Columbo, Hill Street Blues, Mod Squad, Kojak, Hawaii Five-O,* and *In the Heat of the Night;* private detective series, *Magnum P.I., Remington Steele, Moonlighting, Mannix, The Rockford Files, Longstreet, Burke's Law, Hawaiian Eye, Surfside Six;* and series chronicling what one might call private sources of protection and justice, *Superman* and *The Green Hornet, The A Team,* and *The Equalizer.* There have been series on the FBI and various intelligence services: *The Untouchables, I Spy, Man from U.N.C.L.E.,* and *MacGyver.* There have been PBS adaptations of the mystery novels of Arthur Conan Doyle, Margery Allingham, and P. D. James and spy novels by John Le Carré. The same dramas of the pursuit of justice and the action of law have been set in the West: *Gunsmoke, Wyatt Earp, Wild, Wild West, Wanted: Dead or Alive, Kung Fu,* and *The Lone Ranger.*[6] The constancy of the action of the law and of the dilemmas of the pursuit of justice establishes an apparent ideological unity that transcends history.

Law is granted a kind of primacy on television—in the frequency of shows concerning it, and within the scripts of particular episodes. Many series foster respect for the police, for intelligence agencies, for lawmen. They present their protagonists as admirable people, with intelligence, a sense of duty, affecting human weaknesses, and often superhuman powers. Yet even the most adulatory series commonly confront challenges to this portrayal of the agents of the law, with episodes concerning police corruption and characters whose abilities or morality are inferior to the principals'. The presumption of competence and dedication that undergirds police shows like *Hill Street Blues* is countered by private eye series that presume official incompetence or inadequacy, or those, like *Sea Hunt, Hart to Hart,* or *Murder She Wrote,* in which individuals without official standing are placed (with a frequency that does not even pretend to be credible) in circumstances that require them to intervene. There are series, too, that mock the institutions others laud. Television sets *Get Smart* against *I Spy* and *The Man from U.N.C.L.E.,* the goofiness of *Night Court* against the gravity of *Perry Mason* and *L.A. Law,* a straight-faced *Superman* against the self-parodic glee of *Batman.*

The traditional revolutionary admiration and affection for the outlaw shows itself even in those series where the protagonists represent the law. Police officers on television, like Dirty Harry Callahan in the movies, Robin Hood in folklore, and the Founding Fathers in rebellion, often do justice by breaking the law. Their transgressions mark them as the agents not merely of the law but of justice. This distinction becomes clearer still in those series and episodes where the forces of law become the agents of injustice: *The Fugitive* and (in a lighter vein) *The A Team.*

Television accepts, and in accepting contributes to, the prominence of law and the professions of the law in American political culture. Yet this acceptance is not uncritical. Television draws the viewer's eye to the distinction between law and justice and marks the former as inferior. The law emerges as a privileged medium for the pursuit of justice, but no more. The pursuit of justice is marked as an enterprise distinct from the enforcement of the law, accomplished sometimes through, sometimes despite, the law's agents. The establishment of justice is treated on television as it is in the Constitution, as an object sought by the people before, as well as in, the establishment of the law.

The ambivalence of Americans before the law, at once critical and deferential, hailing it as the means for the pursuit of justice and marking its distinction from that higher object, pervades American canonical documents and American popular culture. It is perhaps not surprising then to see elements of that complexly articulated ambivalence in the workings of the law itself.

Legal Representation

The law is a vast construction of representations. It is a representation of an aspect of the common good and the collective will, fashioned by representative legislators. The trial is, in form and issue, a drama of representation. Those who come before the law are represented by counsel and in the records of the trial. They may represent interests and ends beyond their own. They will present contending representations of the facts of the case.

It is often said (most often by lawyers) that "he who represents himself has a fool for a client." What is most striking about this statement is not its commentary on the wisdom of choosing to represent oneself but the structures of law the truism captures. One must be represented, whether by oneself or another. No one comes before the court as oneself. Those who choose to represent themselves exploit that splitting of the self on which the state depends. They may be peculiarly privy to the experience, the memories, and the intentions of their clients, but they will find little advantage in this. They will be bound, as any other would be bound, to represent their clients in literary form, creating for the court a representation of their client's actions and intentions that accords with the law.

Both parties who come before the court are represented. If there are more than two, they will nevertheless be represented as two, "defense" and "prosecution," or "plaintiff" and "defendant." They are invested with a legal identity derived from their place in the structure of litigation.

In criminal trials, one of the parties will be the state. It is here that representation is most fully exploited, for the state is represented many times, and in many forms, in the criminal trial. The defendant is apprehended by the state in one capacity, warned, charged, and prosecuted by the state in several others. Each representation of the state contains others within it. Thus the police who represent a city, county, or state may momentarily represent the nation in the apprehension of federal offenders. In informing those arrested of their rights they represent a consciousness of the Constitution. They represent not only several of the institutions that structure the state but also certain of its diverse capacities. In any criminal trial the state manifests itself in several representatives. The judge, the jury, the prosecuting attorney, the police, and public defenders all represent institutions, offices, capacities, powers, and functions of the state.

The fragmentation of the state in such trials reveals rarely acknowledged facets of representative government. The diverse representations of the state manifest and reify the structure of the state, and the diverse interests, powers, and limitations that follow from it. Where one aspect of the state is pitted against another, one may see a representation of institutional identity and interests, and the conflicts to which these give rise. Beneath these bureaucratic disputes, one may discern the contradictions in the state that these institutional conflicts order and express. The diverse ends and interests of the police, the prosecuting attorney, and the public defender illustrate the conflicts engendered by the rationalization of state functions and relations. The diverse structures, styles, ends, and inclinations of judge and jury indicate an ambivalence in representative government between the desire for justice and adherence to procedure. The process of rationalization, in the articulation of the judicial process, institutionalizes contradictions inherent in the state.

The state comes to the law divided in itself. The Constitution promises to establish justice. The constituted nation continues to pursue, through law, the justice it has not seen fully established.[7] The courts are not simply, or not yet, the province of justice. They are charged, as Supreme Court justices have reminded us of late, not with securing justice but with determining the law. If a law is unjust, they cannot alter or amend it. If a law, otherwise just, secures in some instance an unjust result, they are not empowered to set it momentarily aside.[8] The structure of the American regime marks the distinction between law from justice many times in the structure of the state.

The fragmentation of the state suggests a cultural adherence to a kind of perspectivism. It is understood that conflicts between branches of government, or (within a branch) between obligations, powers, and ends of the state, are more than artifacts of private interest realized and pursued in an institutional context. The policeman whose zeal for enforcement inclines him to laxity in conforming to laws and regulations and the governor who pardons a convicted criminal are not invariably regarded as doing so merely to further a narrow conception of their interest or that of their office. They may even be portrayed, like John Altgeld, or, for that matter, "Dirty Harry" Callahan, as heroes. Such portrayals do more than acknowledge the distance between law and justice, or the presence in the culture of diverse opinions on which ends and activities should have primacy. The portrayals invite the recognition that these diverse opinions are the consequence of contradictions that constitute the state, and that their presence is not an aberration but an inevitability. Within a single state, regard for the citizens in their singularity, in their collectivity, for the ends of the collective and the structures that realize it, entail mutually constitutive, but nevertheless contradictory, perspectives. The acknowledgment of their common legitimacy supports rather than subverts the constitution of the collective.

In law, it is not only the parties to the dispute that are (many times) represented but the dispute itself. At the center of litigation is the creation of a convention that will serve as currency for truth. With this, as with other such conventions, the convention is privileged over the truth it purports to represent. In order to be justiciable, an event must be represented as a violation of law. The account of "what happened" must be structured by law. Those matters to which the law is indifferent will be muted or go altogether unmentioned. In the course of the trial, contending constructions of the event will be presented, as each party to the dispute attempts to structure "what happened" in a manner that will represent it as acting within the law. These contending accounts may be many times amended, as each party attempts to incorporate (in a manner favorable to itself) elements introduced by the other, or specific laws it did not endeavor to accommodate in its original constructions. Each party, then, offers an interpretation of "what happened." The jury (or the judge) that decides the case will cull from these representations of events its own interpretation of "what happened." This representation, the only one that may go unspoken, is marked as authoritative. Kim Lane Scheppele's writings on the construction of fact in law recognize the exercise of interpretation in their creation and give substance to the too-little-noticed etymological kinship between fact and fiction. Scheppele observes that the process of interpretation pervades both the application of laws to cases and the construction of "the facts in the case." Legal interpretation, she writes, "is not only performed with legal texts like statutes or constitutional clauses. It must also be performed with the seemingly simple statements of what happened." [9]

The recognition that these constructions of the facts are interpretations obliges us to recognize that "the version of facts that courts find to be true in particular cases is not the right or best or only truth." [10] Certainly it is not the only truth, for it is a construction that acknowledges its own partiality. Much of "what happened," though true, concerns things—and personal attributes—to which the law must remain indifferent. It is this quality of the law that led artists to represent it as blind.

In acknowledging the partiality of the determination of the truth in court, we are also obliged to recognize that "those who construct descriptions of fact are engaged in a creative enterprise" and that this, "like other creative enterprises, operates within constraints provided both by the genre and by the standards of evaluation worked out in the discourse of criticism." [11] We are obliged to recognize legal disputes as struggles over authority. Each of the contending parties is engaged in a construction of events, a representation of history. Each endeavors to impose its will on the world, to reconstruct the world in a manner that will further the party's interests and desires. But these interests, these desires, these constructions of past and present are governed by prior constructions. The interests and desires that govern each construction of events are themselves the consequences of earlier constructions of the parties as individuals, citizens, consumers, delinquents. The genre in which these utterances are expressed, the court in which they are heard, are constructions. Behind and before these, the obligation to be represented and to present a representation of events, the manifold representations of the authority of the state, the ascription of final authority to representatives (whether judge or jury) all bespeak the prior establishment of representation as the medium of law, and of authority.

The decision between these contending constructions of events is given, in law, to representatives of the collective—to the judge or jury as representative of the community. The ascription of authority to these is very telling. It is the collective, through the mediation of representation, that is once again structurally invested with the power to establish convention.

The question of which version of events, which construction of the truth, is "right" or "best" is dependent on the criteria used for judgment. Right for what? Best for whom? The structure of the American judicial system gives the determination of these criteria over to the collective. It is the collective that is permitted to serve itself, to select those representations that accord with its ends, interests, and desires. Such decisions are not, however, given to the collective directly. They are mediated by layer upon layer of representation. The decision is given, in the final analysis, not to the collective but to its representation in the court. The distinction is a crucial one, for the conventional criteria that serve to establish what is true not only advance the ends of the polity, they perpetuate the privileging of representation.

Tocqueville's reading of American law, in its marking of lawyers as authoritative, in its emphasis on the formal, conventional, and procedural qualities of law, marks law and lawyers as a countervailing force of democracy. In his construction, law, and the servants of law, are at once in opposition to, and in the service of, democracy, preserving it through contradiction. Tocqueville's reading is extremely discerning, not least in its implicit recognition of contradiction as constitutive. It might incline one, however, to see the American legal system as a structure in which representation has an undisputed, unqualified primacy.

There is much to be said for this construction. It accords with the privileging of procedure, in law as in elections. It draws one's attention to the layers of representation that govern the construction of truth in the courts. But it does not capture the presence of contradictions in the legal system itself. Among the most-interesting features of the legal system are those structures and moments where representation gives way.

The constitutive contradiction in representation, between the representative and the represented, between the present signifier and the absent signified, shows itself throughout the legal system. There are also structures and practices within this system that reveal the fictional character of representation, and call into question the conventional construction of truth.

One of the most conspicuous acknowledgments of law as fiction can be seen in the play of "objections." Lawyers are bound by convention to speak within the law. Certain types of evidence—hearsay, for example, and evidence obtained by illegal means—are inadmissable. Certain strategies of argument—leading the witness, for example—are not permitted. Nevertheless, these may be (judiciously) employed. Lawyers may bring forth evidence and arguments they know will be disallowed, mindful that striking these from the record does not altogether strike them from the minds of even the most legalistic jurors.

Judge and jurors, similarly bound, will be similarly unable to erase these and the other memories that inform their consideration and govern their interpretations of the case. The process of selecting jurors favors those who lack expertise in the law. They are constructed as a body concerned less with form than with content, disinclined to privilege procedure. Though they are representative, though they hear a case mediated by representatives and representation, they are not required to enunciate their own version of "what happened." They are enjoined from publishing the criteria they employ in judging between representations. The procedures whereby they decide their verdict remain unknown to the law and hence ungoverned by it. They can decide the case according to criteria altogether foreign to the law. They can ignore certain of the judge's instructions, and the forms of law. The jury, therefore, offers one avenue for diminishing, if not escaping, the authority of representation in the law. The presence of the jury, and the constitutional reiteration of its importance, imbeds, in the network of representations that will alter and diminish it, an affirmation of the authority of the collective in the establishment of convention.[12]

The tension between form and content, procedure and issue, and the representation and that which it represents also animates controversies over the selection of judges. Selection by appointment, particularly where the appointment is made by a panel of legal experts whose principal criterion is legal expertise, marks a privileging of procedure in the legal process and serves to distance the judiciary from the passions, concerns, and interests of the community. Election of judges marks a relative disregard for procedure. The former process makes the judge a representative of legality; the latter constructs the judge as a representative of a particular community.

The primacy of representation lapses in habeas corpus as well. The blunt injunction to produce the body is altogether antithetical to representation. It declares that representation is inadequate. The construction of a literary persona (the representation of identity—particularly the body—in writing) is marked as fictive and unreliable. It is the material body that must be produced.

It is noteworthy that two of these provisions that protest against the primacy of representation, the right to a trial by jury, and that securing the writ of habeas corpus, are granted particular importance in the Constitution.[13] They figure in the popular ideologies, and histories, of America (and other former British colonies) as a bulwark against tyranny and arbitrary rule. Collective memory speaks, in these institutions, against the truism that procedural regularity precludes arbitrariness.

It is in these contradictions, where representation appears to give way, that representation is most fully realized, for it is in these that representation reveals itself as a lie. The recognition of the lie in representation, that it is what it is not, is also properly a recognition of its truth. Representation depends on contradiction. The contradictions of the judicial system—the unspeaking, ungovernable jury, the writ of habeas corpus, and the play of objections—elaborate the contradictions inherent in representation. Here, where representation is most privileged, and most elaborated, representation is most conspicuously subverted. The recognition that representations are not what they claim to be is the gift of representation itself. The signifier persists; the difference between the sign and what it signifies is evident to the eye, the ear, the mind. One sees a man in the robes of justice, one hears in the play of objections the operation of those procedures that transform disputed memories and partial artifacts into the facts of the case.

It is in the workings of the law that one finds the conventional conception of truth most clearly enunciated. It is in law that one finds the conventions of representation most fully elaborated, most rigorously adhered to. Yet it is in law that one finds a series of practices and institutions that remove final authority from the conventions of representation to the representation of convention.

Subject and Sovereign

Those who come before the law in a trial come not as law's authors but as its subjects. They are partial. Though there are class action suits, these stand as exceptions to the common form in which the single accused confronts the state, or two individuals confront one another before the state. Even those who are accused of having committed a crime together may be (and commonly are) tried separately. In all cases, they are constructed as individuals, separate from the collective and the law—dependent on the first and subject to the second. This singularity is underlined by the common formula: "*The State* v. _____."

Their partiality is again affirmed by the adversarial form of the trial. The stance of neutrality is denied to individuals as it is appropriated by one arm of the state. One must either accuse or defend; one must be plaintiff or defendant before the court. With the separation from the collective, and the ascription of constitutional partiality, comes the ascription of moral partiality.

As citizens are transformed from a collective author to individual subjects, the meaning of speech is inverted as well. In the Declaration, the Constitution, the Bill of Rights, and the ordinary ideology of the nation, speech is the medium of authority, the means for self-determination. Speaking is the condition of the free. Before the law, it is otherwise. Consider the Miranda rules. Here freedom consists not in the right to speak but in the right to remain silent, and to have another (if you wish, one "appointed by the state") to speak for you. Freedom is secured here not by speaking but by being spoken to. It is the officer's spoken caution that secures one's rights, if not one's liberty. One's own speech is conceived here as presenting not the possibility of authority but the danger of self-incrimination. This conception of speech continues to operate in the course of the trial. One cannot be compelled to speak against oneself.

The form of the trial inverts a series of relations central to the constitution, and the ordinary conduct, of American politics. Speech, once the medium of authority, becomes the medium of subjection. Rights once secured by speaking for oneself are here secured by having another speak on one's behalf. In the constitutional speeches of the regime, the people in their common character dictated the state. Here, people in their singularity confront the state's dictates. These inversions enact and elaborate the ambivalence of citizenship, the condition Rousseau describes with elegant brevity in the *Social Contract*, "the words subject and Sovereign are identical correlatives, the idea of which reunites itself under the single word 'citizen'." [14]

The form of the trial manifests the citizen's subjection to the law and the citizen's rights under the law. The citizen appears as subject rather than as author of the law.[15] The architecture of the courtroom reflects the architecture of the trial. Those on trial stand (literally) below the judge. The architectural and procedural forms of the trial construct the individual as partial and singular, weak in the confrontation with the power of the state. The emphasis on subjection to the law in preference to constitutional authority makes the form of the trial relatively more attractive to those who prefer the citizen as subject to the citizen as sovereign.

Hearings and Spectacles

The same procedural, architectural, and dramatic inflection foregrounding the citizen as subject is evident in those quasi-judicial proceedings, congressional hearings. Here, as in judicial trials, those called are brought as individuals before the state in its collective form and power. Even when those called before such committees come with an entourage of lawyers and aides, the hearing continues to present itself—visibly, formally—as a confrontation between the power of the state and an individual: Abbie Hoffman, John Ehrlichman, Oliver North, Clarence Thomas. Even when those called before the committee come as representatives of another branch of the government, they are seen by the press and people as individuals: not the executive branch or the navy but John Poindexter, not the Department of Housing and Urban Development but Samuel Pierce.

Recollections of the 1960s counterpose spectacles to hearings, ·demonstrations to trials, speech (and several other kinds of sound) to silence. Hearings and trials took place in closed rooms, according to strict procedural forms. Demonstrations took place in the open, often against the law, always confronting established forms. In hearings and trials a single individual, or two or three still in the isolation of their individuality, confronted the collective power of the state. In demonstrations, some portion of the people assembled confronted the now-isolated state. In one the people appeared as subjects, in their singularity. In the other they appeared as the assembled Union; they claimed authority. In one silence offered protection. In the other speech was employed as the medium of authority.

Though the Rosenberg trial cast the defendants as the agents of a foreign state, a state (indeed, an empire) committed to collectivization, the cultural artifacts in which we remember the Rosenberg trial emphasize the private character of Ethel and Julius Rosenberg: their marital relations, their letters to one another, their children. The trial bears their name, not the name of the state they served. The McCarthy hearings lost their momentum at the moment they became identified with the private interests of a single man. The army–McCarthy hearings reversed the ordinary economy of the hearings: the committee did not confront General Ralph Zwicker; Joe McCarthy confronted the army.

The demonstrations and spectacles of the 1960s were, of course, accompanied by trials and hearings, yet the participants transformed hearings into spectacles, the trials of individuals into collective displays. When Jerry Rubin was called to testify before the House Un-American Activities Committee, he came first in the dress of a guerrilla, then in the dress of a soldier of an earlier revolution. The trials of the 1960s bear the names of collectives: "The Chicago Seven" and "The Black Panther Trials." Judge Julius Hoffman appeared isolated on the bench, confronted by a united and raucous collective, representative of a larger mob, representative of a still larger movement. The Rosenbergs could not be made to speak, would not confess. The Chicago Seven could not, would not, keep silent. The 1950s are remembered in the silence of the Fifth Amendment, the 1960s in chanting, and in songs. The 1950s are remembered, fondly by some, with more contempt by others, as the decade of social conformity. The 1960s are remembered, fondly by some, with contempt by others, as the decade of rebellion. This contrast between the popular memories of these decades captures how Americans in different historical moments, with different attitudes toward authority, stand before the law.

Speaking and Writing

A curious economy of speaking and writing appears in the form of the trial. In this, the province of the law, where writing has an uncontested primacy, speaking appears to be privileged.

Reading and writing, commonly regarded as the silent, undisturbing pursuits of the pacific and the respectable, are forbidden to those who attend trials. The spectators are constructed as witnesses. They must see the witnesses, the prosecution and defense, the judge and jury, speak, and they must hear their words. The proceedings of the court are spoken. Witnesses, who might testify as thoroughly in writing, are called to the stand and obliged to give their testimony in speech. They begin by taking an oath, aloud. Even those who have submitted depositions are called upon to testify to these in speech. The verdict is given, and the sentence passed, in speech.

Yet all this speaking passes into writing. The court recorder sits without speaking and, as each word is spoken, casts it into writing. The words, indeed, are treated as writing from the moment of the utterance. The listening jury members may be instructed, from time to time, to erase from their minds a statement by a witness, prosecution, or defense. They are treated as if they were engaged in the construction of a common text. So they are. They are engaged in the construction of a text within a text within a text. They, in common with the judge, the prosecution, and the defense, are engaged in constructing the text of the trial.

The text of the trial, when the trial is finished and a verdict rendered, becomes embedded in the text of the law. It must either reaffirm (and in reaffirming alter) or deliberately challenge existing law. In either case the law will be changed: invisibly strengthened, or visibly altered. The speech of the courtroom will have been written into law. This text, the text of the law, is itself embedded in the text of the Constitution, which must be likewise rewritten upon every instance of its application.

The trial, then, does not place speech over writing, as first appeared, nor does it elevate writing over speech. Rather it captures and elaborates that moment in which speech becomes writing. Liberal regimes, as Derrida observes, voice themselves. Each nation marks itself as a "unanimous people assembled in the self-presence of its speech." [16] The American nation called itself into being in the Declaration and called upon the world to witness it. This documented speech is followed in the American canon by another still more authoritative. In the Constitution, as in the Declaration, the American nation speaks itself into being in writing. The practice of the American courts echoes Derrida's conception of speech, where writing is already present in the spoken word.

SIX

Representation
and the Silences
of Politics

A COMPLEX ECONOMY OF SPEAKING AND WRITING, speaking and silence, words and images, makes up—in part—the constitution of politics in linguistic practice. Our practices within this economy, and our understandings of it, are framed by the cultural construction of the practices of speaking and writing. Popular culture and political theory have invested the practices of speaking and writing with political meaning, and established a covert economy of speaking and writing, speaking and silence.

The American regime openly privileges speech. The canonical documents of the regime were cast, for all their writtenness, as speech. The nation was brought forth (so Lincoln spoke of the text) as speech.[1] The Declaration was made, heard, acclaimed. Then it was signed. The Constitution was written in the past as if it were to be spoken in the present.[2]

The privileging of speech follows from the cultural construction of that act. Speech effects and signifies the individual independence and communicative entry into public life central to liberalism. Speech is immediate. It issues from a living body.[3] Speech is said to be the utterance of an internal will, a will otherwise unknown. It is through this expression of an interior, private will that the individual enters into relations with others.

Liberalism, as Derrida observes, sees itself fulfilled in "the self-presence of its speech."[4]

Writing, on the other hand, is cast in popular culture and the academy as the medium of external domination. Max Weber identifies writing with the bureaucracy, bureaucracy with the Iron Cage. The phrases he uses to contrast the dictates of structure with the disruptive power of charismatic moments reiterate the opposition of speaking and writing: "It is written . . . but I say unto you." Scripture, for Weber as for Calvin, sets in motion a concatenation of determinations that end in a polity where self-determination is precluded, where all selves are, indeed, always—and already—determined. Writing is experienced by most people as authority imposed upon them: in religion, in education, in law. They read scriptures, laws, and regulations. They rarely act as authors—or with authority—themselves. They fill out forms and find the answers decided for them. They pay bills and find the act of writing effects not the extension of the self but the loss of property. Commonplace condemnations of red tape and the bureaucracy, of restrictions and regulations, express the quotidian experience of writing as an imposed authority.

Liberalism, for all its privileging of speech, depends on writing as well. Rousseau's democracy fulfills itself in the people assembled—the present citizenry, speaking its mind.[5] Yet behind the speech of the citizenry is the writing of the legislator. For all its valorized dependence on utterance, on expression in the word, liberalism depends on strategic silences. Locke's construction of consent in practice turns upon a reading of silence. It is in the silence of the people that one reads their consent to the regime.

Reading the Written in Speech

In this context, the economy of the word seems to alternately hold out and withdraw a promise. The founding of the political order in speech promises self-determination and the legitimation of the regime through the immediacy of spoken consent. This speech, the realm of freedom, is replaced by writing, the instrument of rule, the order of authority. Yet writing holds out the hope of reproducing the freedoms promised by speech. The forms of the American regime argue for the presence of consent, of self-determination, despite the rigors of political order, in the preservation of speech in writing. Writing holds out promises as well. The lie of writing enables constitutional regimes to construct themselves in an ideal, scriptural form that transcends past or present defects. In his speech at the Lincoln Memorial, Martin Luther King referred to the Constitution as a promissory note that had yet to be redeemed. In this contemporary instance of what Sacvan Bercovitch terms "the American jeremiad," speech recalled the promises of writing, restoring them to an authoritative place in contemporary political debates. Here too, however, it is speech that serves to realize the promise of self-determination.

This promise is challenged by the reading of writing in speech. Where speech is constructed as the medium of self-determination, writing as the medium of an imposed authority, the recognition of speech as written threatens to erase the possibility of self-determination entirely. The spectre of the Iron Cage haunts liberals who read the texts of Hans Georg Gadamer, Michel Foucault, Elias Canetti, Paul Ricoeur, and Jacques Derrida.[6]

When these writers read writing in speech, they raise the possibility that "the words speak for themselves" in a sense quite different from the liberal understanding of speech. The transparency of meaning and intention and the coincidence of utterance and will that the phrase evokes are answered by an echo, reflecting and opposing it. The words speak not for the speaker but for themselves. They have authority over the one who utters them. One who experiences, desires, feels pain, and then recasts these—in thought or utterance—into words casts an inchoate sensation into an already-defined form. It is through these words that the sensation is understood. The words author not only our utterances of ourselves but our interior understanding of our experience, sentiments, and desires. Writing is present and active, therefore, not merely in speech but prior to speech, in thought. Rather than merely supplying the self with a means of utterance, words mediate the self's understanding of itself. They are constitutive of private, as well as public, identity. As thought is cast into words and uttered in speech the already-alienated sentiments of the speaking subject are further removed. As these words are heard by others, they escape the speaker's authority. They will be invested with meaning and effects foreign to the speaker's intention. They become part of a public discourse in which the speaker is bound with others. If the subject writes, or these spoken words are recorded in writing, the words are alienated not only from the speaker but from those who heard them spoken—those who, in hearing them, invested them with meaning and effects. They are alienated from the context in which they were spoken. They are made to transcend their time and place. Translation and interpretation—by readers, ethnographers, political analysts—impel successive moments of alienation and transcendence. At each remove, the speech is alienated from the speaker. At each remove, the speaker is bound within a larger communicative community. At each remove, the speech, acquiring additional meaning and effects, extends its own significance and authority, and the significance and authority of the speaker. Power and subjection, community and alienation, are inextricably linked within this process for each is the condition of the other. The ambivalence of this process is lost in the construction of speaking as freedom, writing as domination. Yet despite the conspicuous interplay of speaking and writing in the mythology of American constitution, acceptance of this rigid dichotomy and a determined inattention to the linguistic turn in philosophy continue to dominate liberal theory.[7]

Liberal theorists fear the recognition of the written in speech. If one sees speech as written, one sees the text as veil.[8] Meaning and will lose the shared transparency they were ascribed. If we cannot see clearly through the words to the will, consent is compromised. If words speak not simply for the speaker but for themselves, if our sentiments are written for us, in us, before we speak, then the words we hear are not simply the speech of the subject but the speech of subjection.

In reading the silent texts of speech we discover the silences of the speaker. Those who initially appeared as the authors of their words now reveal themselves as authored by them: constituted in language. The words that once appeared as the means for a singular and pristine interiority to impose itself on the external political world now reveal themselves as the medium through which the external world imposes itself—before speech, before thought—on those who live in language.

Liberals—and romantic existentialists—identified self-expression and self-discovery with liberation. Their enterprise was predicated on the notion of an autonomous self, an independent will that the individual could discover within. Freud's writings reveal the impossibility of such an enterprise. The self was necessarily constituted as such in a cultural framework; it was dependent upon, and followed from, a political order.[9] The heresies of psychology could, however, be assimilated (through translation) to the demands of liberalism. Successful efforts identified the ego with the self and mandated the restraint of passion (now, the id) and the avoidance of external tyranny (now, the superego) in a long-familiar economy. Psychoanalysis became "the talking cure," and Freud another partisan of the discovery of the self and the reconciliation of the world through speech.

Freud could be assimilated, bowdlerized. Lacan was more difficult. The referential and structural density of Lacan's elegant prose secured it against the dangers of too facile a reading. Lacan reaffirms the priority of the political order. In this he follows Nietzsche's recognition that "we are all philologists now," conscious of ourselves as being in language. The self at the core of the self, the will, was neither autonomous nor singular. It lacked integrity, and it lacked boundaries.[10] It was created under the authority of language.

In speaking of that which speaks silently in speech, we began to articulate the inscription of authority on the subjected speaker. Reading what is written in speech reveals covert and unacknowledged, unvoiced, structures of governance and constitution. Hegel ascribes determinative power to those constitutive categories in which we find ourselves. Prior to consciousness, they were nevertheless the occasion for it. Prior to the self, they were nevertheless the means for its realization. Gadamer's account of our being in language likewise affirms the value of established categories: the virtue, in his words, of prejudice. Althusser's account of hailing, or "interpellation," on the other hand, is concerned entirely with the coercive effects of these constructions. Foucault's revelatory readings of those cultural constructions we took to be most natural—reason, sexuality, and the shape of knowledge—are likewise recognitions of this silent coercion.

Those who recognized, with Hegel and Gadamer, Nietzsche and Lacan, our deep indebtedness to established categories and conditions saw the enterprise of self-determination, self-discovery, as simultaneously individual and collective, uniting public and private constitution in the recognition of a common genealogy. Those who looked, like Althusser and Foucault, for deliverance from coercive structures found them in the very constitution of the self. The recognition of subjection written into the speaking subject recasts, indeed replaces, the liberal struggle for liberation. The recognition of the self, no longer an apolitical and ahistorical enterprise, becomes an activity of political comprehension. For those who would remake themselves, the task becomes, in Foucault's words, "not to discover who we are, but to refuse who we are." [11]

Reading the silent texts of speech entailed a revision of the assumption of the pristine interiority of the will on which liberalism was based. It revealed the presence of domination within the self, and the subjection of the will to language. The recognition of the subjection of all people to language brought with it notice of the presence of an aspect of being outside language.

Silence about being outside of language, if such there is, is necessary and inescapable. Silence about being in language, on the contrary, is silence of our own volition. The silence of the will and experience of the subjected in speech is preserved by the silence about the authority of language. The recognition that the political order inscribes itself upon our thoughts before we speak, even before we think—that in speech we are always, already, part of the political order—extends the reach of political thought and reveals new fields of political action and analysis. The repeated dismissal of those who recognized the constitutive power of language as apolitical is therefore inappropriate, if not disingenuous. [12] It is a silence with strategic implications.

Silence concerning the authority of language over the constitution of the self, the realization and expression of the will, permits liberal regimes to maintain the myth of the word, particularly the spoken word, as a neutral instrument for the utterance and realization of the individual will. It enables liberal regimes to maintain established hierarchies by predicating the achievement of equality and the establishment and maintenance of cultural difference on involvement in practices that obstruct or preclude these ends.

Strategic Speech, Strategic Silences

Liberal theories and liberal therapies commonly turn on the neutrality of language. Negotiation is recommended as if all were rendered equal in speech, as if it were an instrument that would serve any hand.[13] Yet those nominally neutral words are inscribed with diverse systems of domination.[14] Hierarchies of class and race, of gender and regional difference, are written into language. Often, they can be heard in speech. Differences of accent and dialect, of idiom and word choice, mark the speaker. Even if one were to speak from behind a veil, these would inscribe identity. They convey not only identity but a place in hierarchies of identity. They inscribe inequality: advantaging some, disadvantaging others.

Where dialogue reiterates already-established identities and hierarchies, equality may be better served by silence. Where speech inscribes inferiority, silence may refuse it. Yet the refusal of speech with another is read, in liberal theory and in popular culture, not as the refusal of subordination but as a refusal of equality. The mythic construction of speech as the expression of a self secured from politics in the confines of an open mind and a closed body reiterates the identification of speech with freedom and equality.

Dialogue, where speech is so constructed, becomes difficult if not impossible to refuse. Refusal is read as the denial of a voice to another, as the denial of another's rights. The demand for dialogue is often, however, coercive in itself.

The obligation to talk with those one would reject imposes an obligatory community where none may be desired, giving the lie to consent and the tolerance of difference. Coerced participation in dialogue, coerced speech, is presented as an invitation to self-expression and equality, yet those who are brought into these against their will have already been denied one aspect of their self-determination. They enter subordinate.

Those whose inequality is written into language will find themselves doubly subordinated, in the course of the dialogue as well as in their concession to it. They will be at a disadvantage in this medium and experience this putative freedom as subjection. They will be obliged to listen once again to those whose voices are already heard, to give airtime and houseroom to the already dominant. They are obliged by the forms of negotiation to concede to the dominant the very conditions they combat.

The construction of dialogue as obligatory gives strategic advantage to the dominant culture, which is thereby enabled to intrude itself into every space. Instances of this can be found in the most commonplace dimensions of popular culture and political discourse. The column "Hers" in the magazine section of the Sunday *New York Times* alternates with "About Men" in an affirmation of equality in symmetry that denies the preference given to men, male activities, and male interests in the remainder of the paper. White students excluded from black student groups who charge "reverse discrimination" make the same strategic assumption of symmetry, denying the exclusion of blacks and African-American culture in (only) nominally neutral organizations throughout the university. The exclusion of whites from African-American groups and activities does not deny them a voice. They are given a voice in every medium, and virtually every venue. Their inclusion, however, denies expression to an African-American voice, which cannot be heard elsewhere.

The demands by the already included, indeed, the already privileged, for inclusion, for further speech and "equal opportunity," depend for their force on a denial of history. The presence of the past in institutional structures, in meanings inscribed on bodies, gestures, and images, confers power—and the access to power—discriminately. The individual is a being prior to history and culture, with rights consequent on that condition. Yet these individuals are also embedded in history, with the privileges (or burdens) consequent on that condition. This ambivalence in the constitution of individuals in the world makes possible the strategic denial of individual rights through claims made on the basis of those rights.

Efforts to maintain special privilege, derived less from history than from structural power, may employ a similarly strategic denial. In such strategies, the exercise or extension of a privileged position in the structures of institutional power is disguised as the exercise of a common right. The erasure of structural power is most evident in claims made by public officials that they have been denied their right to speak when they are interrupted by heckling or drowned out by the audience. Consider the case in its most common form. The official denied a voice at that time possesses the ability to be heard elsewhere. The press will invariably print the speech (or any comment the official wishes to make) in its entirety. The official, moreover, possesses the means to be heard should the press not extend this service. The official is denied not speech but a hearing—in that place, at that time, to that audience. It is hardly an unusual condition. Few of us can find a hearing where and when we wish it, before the audience of our choosing. What is denied to the official, therefore, is not the right to speech but the enjoyment of deference.

The conditions of the nominal denial impugn it further. The official stands apart, surrounded by the trappings of power: an entourage, often including police or security people, a podium, and a microphone. The official speaks and is interrupted, heckled perhaps, drowned out by boos or calls from the crowd. The official's speech depends upon their silence. Their speech silences his. The question in such an instance is thus not "Will they deny him a hearing?" but rather "Who will be heard here?"

Law may dictate deference to officials, elected or appointed. Convention may prescribe more deference to one who stands at the podium than one who stands below it. Reason will prefer reflection to recitation and deliberation to abuse—a preference that may (or may not) prove to the advantage of the official. Regard for the right to speak, however, does not entail deference on those who assemble. The imposition of silence upon them, whether by convention or by force, denies the very freedom it purports to defend and disguises the exercise of an extended authority as the exercise of a right.

Context is critical to the economy of expression in another respect as well. The expression of views, or the assumption of identities acceptable to the dominant culture, will entail no costs. They may indeed bring advantage with them, as those in positions of power are able to identify individuals possessing traits procedures would prevent them from observing. Freedom of expression is not, however, free for the subaltern or the dissident. The experiences of dissent and agreement in a room where one view is dominant differ dramatically. The woman who makes public her abortion, the man who announces that he's gay, will pay, often heavily, in private as well as public life, for their use of the freedom of speech.

Demands for negotiation may be similarly deceptive. As participation in dialogue may effectively deny to the subaltern the full expression that speech purportedly secures to all, so demands for negotiation may make possible strategies of covert repression. Recourse to negotiation may silence mass movements that speak in action rather than in words. Actions, and the collective speech of signs and chants, songs and gestures, are replaced with a conversation between nominally representative individuals. The replacement of collective action—often disordered, subject to continual changes in organization and tactics—with conventionally governed, highly structured negotiations deprives insurrectionary movements of one of their principal strategic advantages: the capacity for surprise. The identification and installation of representatives of the mass movement reifies (where it does not establish) hierarchies and may deprive aspects of the movement of a voice. Finally, and most importantly, replacing collectives with individuals entails acquiescence to the construction of systems of representation as transparent and authoritative. It depends upon and reinforces the liberal model of politics as between individuals rather than collectives.

Words and Images

Speech is valorized in the political mythology of liberal politics and the academy, but writing serves as the privileged medium in each. The primacy of the medium of writing in scholarship, politics, and the bureaucracy reveals their common genealogy—the derivation of the academy from the monastery, of clerks from clerics. The myths of writing and speech, and the practices of conversation, debate, oratory, legislation, legal opinions, books, articles, and reports, meet in a common privileging of the word. There is resistance in politics and the academy to the examination of audible, visible, legible signs other than the word.

The Image and History

The image derives its power from its economy. Concentrated in each image is a dense sediment of reference. Where stereotypes are well established, and the recollected cultural constructions have a long history, a mere gesture—a shuffle or a roll of the eyes—may be enough to call up an entire lexicon of subordination. Perhaps the most-striking instance of this is the image of the woman. There is no visible part of the woman's body that has not been made a sign of her subjection. Any picture of a woman, any of a plethora of feminine gestures, the citation of any of the numberless portrayals of women in the patriarchal lexicon, carries this dense text of subjecting references with it. Contemporary controversies over the representation of women's bodies—in advertising, in pornography, in antiabortionists' display of the contents of their wombs—alternatively challenge and reiterate the meanings inscribed upon the bodies of women. The debate over the woman's body is the debate over a site of authority.

The bodies of African-Americans are likewise inscribed with a history of subjection. Those who would argue, symmetrically, against black racism and white racism must first confront the radical asymmetry in the language of the image. Blackface is a mimic mockery of blackness. Whiteface is mime.[15] The exaggeration of features common to racist caricatures of African-Americans can find no correspondingly racist exaggeration of features of whites. There are no gestures, no caricatures, that subject whites to a mockery they recognize.

The image is characteristically conservative in its referential density. It derives its evocative power from the presence of an already-established lexicon of images and gestures. The historicity and referential density of the image gives credence to Roland Barthes's initially implausible and apparently partisan contention that mythology is the province of the right.[16] Certainly Barthes's denial of a mythology of revolution, with its implicit construction of an unmediated materiality, is implausible. His deprecation of a mythology of the left might seem equally suspect. There is, as Eric Hobsbawm notes, the mythology of banditry, with its subversive discourse on property.[17] There is the mythic Harlem of Langston Hughes, the folk mythology about John Henry, the populist mythology of Vachel Lindsay's poetry, and the persistent popular distrust of big business and the power of the rich. What Barthes recognizes, however, is that though the dense fabric of culture with its contradictions, alternatives, variants, affirmations, and resistances has a place for a mythology of the left that place remains on the margins, in the interstices. The dissident can—and have—appropriated aspects of the dominant culture to argue, mythically, for its subversion, yet they are hampered in such arguments by the inseparability of these myths from a history and a mythic frame that entails the dissident's reaffirmation of their marginality.

Those whom history has advantaged are served by it on several planes. They are advantaged in their status and possessions, in the conscious exercise of institutional power, and in the unconscious enjoyment of a mythic authority. History imbeds acknowledgment of their power in the mythic as well as the institutional structures that govern the subaltern. Literary and imaginary artifacts, like their material and institutional counterparts, bear the marks of their systems of origin. The inequalities that are inscribed in their genealogies inform their use.

The Silence of the Image

The economy of speech and silence in the employment of the image gives it a perverse ambivalence. It is "not only its power but its lack of power that matters."[18] The image speaks, and it conveys meaning, yet it lacks a voice. "Statues and dioramas do not move, nor do they scream or whimper."[19] They cannot convey to us the fullness of the experience, the sentiments, the will they represent. The image of Willie Horton speaks stridently to us, but it does not speak, in any sense, for itself. The Barbie doll and the face or lips or hands of a woman pictured in an advertisement or a piece of pornography speak the texts that have been written upon those bodies. They speak of women, not for them. Women are silent in them.

Yet these images, in their silences, their partiality, convey not only something less but something more. The "inherent inadequacy of the image," its separation from that which is represented, joins the image to others: other images, other people, other contexts, other meanings, other discourses.[20] The partiality of the image is (as the word has it) also its superfluity. The act of representation invests the image with surplus value, if you will; it is its supplement.[21] What is lost is the voice of the represented. What is added are the texts of authority.

It is this economy of meaning that persuades me to refuse. Baudrillard's term *simulacrum*. These representations are not, as Baudrillard's description of the simulacrum suggests, divested of meaning, unconnected to history. They are continually invested with it. Nor are these representations readily emptied of the meanings they convey. It is difficult indeed to detach racist meanings from the image of Willie Horton.[22] These images are constantly transformed, as all signs are, but not with the ubiquitous rapidity that Baudrillard ascribes them. On the contrary, it is the persistence of racist meanings in the image when other discursive systems have been transformed that gives the imagery of racism its strategic importance. It is this property that enables people to speak silently, legibly, and persistently for systems of subordination they nominally denounce.

The inscription of history upon the image gives a distinctive asymmetry to the imaginary strategies available to the powerful and the subaltern. When the powerful employ images of their own power, these images speak both of and for them. The asymmetry is still more striking when the subaltern serve as author. Images of the powerful by the subaltern continue to affirm the title of the powerful to power. History invests the images with remembered cruelties and excesses perhaps but also with remembered power and remembered praise. Images of the subaltern by the subaltern will, conversely, protest against any power they claim. They will recall silently, persistently, a history of slights, powerlessness, and degradation. History thus tends to deny authority—literary and political—to those who have not had it, and to secure it most tenaciously in the hands of those who have held it longest.

This delineation of the economy of speaking and silence, of authority and subjection, in the language of images might seem to recommend that the subaltern reject imagery altogether. This is, of course, as impossible as any other rejection of language. The subaltern will be spoken of—and will speak—in images whether they wish to or not. The recollection of history in the image ensures, moreover, that they will also speak silently and unwillingly for their continued subjection. Such speech need not, however, be uncontested.

Elements of popular culture suggest that the inherently conservative character of the image can be employed for its subversion. As John Fiske and others observe, Madonna and the wannabes employ a lexicon of traditional feminine subordination as a weapon and a means of profit and advancement. Eddie Murphy's recollections of Buckwheat, of the figure of the black pimp, and of the traits ascribed to inner city blacks recalled racial stereotypes, but they were unmistakably disdainful.[23] In presenting these images as laughable, Murphy enlisted the audience in a common rejection of the meaning the image conveys. The success of such strategies turns on the ability of the audience to recognize ridicule, to read mimicry where they might read imitation or enactment. Context is decisive in this. These images are multiply framed, and each frame presents instructions for their reading. There are contextual clues in the presentation. In his portrayal of Buckwheat, for example, Murphy furnished (in subtitles) transliterations of Buckwheat's speech, marking its distance from the black English it purportedly reproduced.

Subaltern groups, if they are to speak for themselves, must employ strategies that permit them to reveal, challenge, mock, and refute that which speaks silently of and against them in the image. They have learned, and often deftly employ, the old Socratic strategy of irony, parody, mimicry, mockery, and a careful ambiguity. Critical readings, directed at giving voice to the silent language of the image, are necessary for the self-determination of the subaltern and any approach to political equity.

Silence about the Image

The conventions of political discourse have opened writing to dialogue. Written words are challenged, debated, opposed, supported, expanded, and responded to as if they were speech. They are read; they are critiqued. Though we employ visual images as forms of communication on a daily basis, the possibility that these forms might be employed, like words, in response to one another, that one might propose alternatives, amend or deny assertions, contradict or refute statements made in the language of images, seems arcane and improbable. In politics and the academy words are the medium of dialogue, and the image remains the possession of history, ceded to the status quo.

169

In "The Meaning of Ethical Neutrality," Weber argues that social scientists should keep silent their political partisanship. "In view of the fact that certain value-questions which are of decisive political significance are permanently banned from university discussion, it seems to me to be only in accord with the dignity of a representative of science to be silent as well about such value-problems as he is allowed to treat."[24] Speech, Weber recognizes, serves established powers and conventions. Silence serves these as well. The refusal, in politics and the academy, to speak of that which speaks silently in speech, wordlessly in the image, runs counter to the vocations, coupled in our discipline, of politics and science.

Popular practice, however, has refused to grant dictatorial powers to the image. Each of us, in dressing everyday, manipulates a complex system of signs conveying information on class, gender, occupation, politics. We read these signs in the clothing of others. We affirm, challenge, and mock them.[25] We do so in the language of words and in the languages provided for us in commodities. In our mastery of this common vernacular we have the rudiments, unconscious and inchoate, of a more thoughtful and more thorough examination of the politics of language.

Democratic Excesses

DEMOCRATIC PRACTICES SUGGEST the presence of an uncele-
brated, even unacknowledged, virtue in democracy. The spirit
that says, "it would be enough for us," is the spirit of religion, captured in its awe at a generous Providence. The spirit
of democracy, always engaged in a struggle to surpass its creators, is of another kind. Democracy is always wanting something. The virtue of democracy lies in its unrest, in its desire
for more.

Democracy cannot be still, cannot be content, cannot be
satisfied. If there is a problem, a solution must be found. If there
is no problem, improvements must be made. In the midst of
these improvements, there is the search for the new. Progress,
the discovery of solutions, invention, and exploration are accompanied by the proliferation of goods, a constant increase of
things, and the constant change of color and form. The drive to
see more, to learn more, to have more, to move a little farther
and a little faster, seems to impel Americans a little further into
infinity.

The inventiveness of democracy is the impulse of the demiurge: to make light in the darkness, to speak to one another
across seas and continents, to fly, to take on all the faculties that
Nature's God denied us. Invention comes, in democracy, not   **171**

from need but from the unrestrained play of the mind and the senses, the reaching ambition of desire.

The desire for more things is the desire, in this republic of signs, for more speech, for more selves. The things we make, the things we buy, present and represent us in the world. Commodities speak of and speak for us. We speak through and in them. We make aspects of ourselves visible to one another. In the crafting of commodities into self-expressions we make our appearances our avatars.

The creation of visible, legible selves in commodities is paralleled by the composition of literary selves. Conscious of our limits in the flesh, we will ourselves to live beyond our bodies, in the nation and in our own words. We accomplish, in the public sphere and private automachia, our own transubstantiation. These literary selves, subject to different limits, endowed with different capacities, become citizens, sovereign and subject, of the republic of signs.

The translation of citizens and nation from flesh to word, from word to flesh, takes many forms. The documentation—private and public—of the citizen is that citizen's deconstruction: the records of ancestry, family, friendship and affinities, skills and defects, successes and failures; a taxonomy of objective traits; an articulation of will and passion, ends and desires. The enactment of the Constitution in the structures of government and the practices of the people is its deconstruction as well, detailing the diverse capacities and faculties of government.

These selves, likewise composed of materials not wholly subject to the will of the author, offer the possibility of representations that are enduring and transcendent. Our desire to give ourselves, singly and collectively, a form that transcends the limits of the flesh is one expression, one instance, one moment of lack and desire.

Democrats attempt to live not only beyond the body but more fully within it. We value, in practice, not only the useful products of the mind but inventions that serve the senses. We can hear more, in changing rhythms and diverse musical styles—jazz pieces, symphonies, rap, and house—in the discovery of electronic sounds and foreign instruments. We can see more: in seasonal changes in color and pattern, the rediscovery of old prints, and the creation of new ones. New sensations in the mouth—bite, sparkle, bitterness, new combinations of flavors—proliferate. We can taste change, and in tasting change, we change, for with each new cuisine comes a new aesthetic. With smell the play of the senses in the world becomes a play with time as well, linking people to their pasts, linking us as a people to a past that was once foreign to us. New scents revive old memories. In the proliferation of fragrances, in finding new uses for them, a seemingly frivolous, seemingly momentary fashion revives an art that was old in the Heian period.

The American passion for expansion—from the Atlantic to the Pacific, to new frontiers, "where no one has gone before"— is allied to a passion to extend ourselves in time. Americans delve into the past, seeking like the Mormons (that most American of religions) to recover lost ancestors and comprehend them in the present community. The past is brought before us in written histories and commercial enterprises: books and films, museums and theme parks. These invite us to enter a past that time would close to us. These representations of the past render it present, accessible, tangible, yet in their multiplicity they apprise us of their partial and constructed character.

The Constitution preserves one moment of that past, but the moment it preserves is the moment of founding. In this moment, the preservation of the past and the imagination of the future become one. The Constitution comprises many such contradictions. Speech is preserved in writing. People yet unborn are made authors of a text they have yet to read. Americans stand before the law as legislators and as outlaws perpetually caught in the act. In this text, a constitution, the sign and security of limited government, is prefaced with a litany of ambitious, if not impossible, imperatives. We call upon ourselves to establish justice.

The contradictions of the Constitution prefigure the generous and demanding practices of popular culture. There is never enough for democrats. Against satisfaction, popular culture speaks of desire: the desire for more things, more knowledge, more sensation, more speech, more forms for the self, more time, more power, more rights, more justice.

Against calculation, popular culture calls for invention: the calculation of profit and loss is countered in practice with the proliferation of uncounted things, sensations, and meanings; against the parsimony of accounting, popular culture advances the generosity of invention. Theory calls for the liberal individual. Practice calls forth the democratic demiurge—making more things, more forms for the self, collectively engaged in the construction of a new world order. Americans look—adventurously, aggressively, evangelically, arrogantly—at boundaries as frontiers. This is a nation extending over land, across oceans, into space; acquiring more territory, more power, more influence, more people, more cultures; transgressing the boundaries of time with those of space; extending itself into past and future; acquiring more histories; comprehending more; making more futures accessible. Recalling, perhaps, a constitutive transgression, Americans refuse the limits of the law for an open constitution: open to question, open to amendment, open to interpretation. The fiction of a polity preserved is countered by the practices of a people open to change, still becoming what they are.

The practices of a liberalism triumphant in the commonplace points to the capacity of democracy to exceed itself. If we look for a democratic ethic, we should look for the ethic suited to its virtues, an ethic of excess, an ethic that asks for more. Lack is the origin, desire the proper impulse, of democracy. Magnanimity is its peculiar virtue.

174

Introduction

1. Jacques Derrida, *Of Grammatology,* trans. Gayatri Chakravorty Spivak (Baltimore: Johns Hopkins University Press, 1976), p. 145. Readers familiar with this concept will recognize that I take considerable liberties with it.

Chapter One

1. This last phrase is taken from George Steiner's essay "Our Homeland, the Text," *Salmagundi* 66 (Winter-Spring 1985): 4–25. In it I imply an affinity between Americans and Jews, in each case, children of the covenant.

2. Umberto Eco, *Travels in Hyperreality,* trans. William Weaver (New York: Harcourt Brace Jovanovich, 1986), p. 6.

3. Ibid., p. 7.

4. Friedrich Nietzsche, *The Use and Abuse of History,* trans. Adrian Collins (New York: Bobbs Merrill, 1957), p. 23.

5. Walter Benjamin, "The Work of Art in the Age of Mechanical Reproduction," in *Illuminations* (New York: Schocken Books, 1969), pp. 220–21. The persistence of the idea of authenticity in the literature must constitute my apology for discussing it. As my friend and colleague Jim Henson observed, "It's a dead jam."

6. Eco, *Travels in Hyperreality,* pp. 6–7.

7. The most common of these stuffed toys is the ubiquitous teddy bear, a representation of one of the more-threatening American predators. Its name associates it, moreover, with an aggressive president, a creature that the institutions and ideology of the American regime endeavor to tame.

8. I recently received, imbedded in a sweepstakes sponsored by

Publishers Clearinghouse, an advertisement (and order form) for one of these devices. It provided a splendid example of another aspect of the ideology of representative government: the identification of the process with the product it is nominally intended to produce. The little box was said to help you win the lottery by enabling you to choose your number *exactly the same way* the lottery computers do: randomly.

9. I am grateful to Vera Zolberg for giving me her insights into corporate influence on the arts. See her *Constructing a Sociology of the Arts* (New York: Cambridge University Press, 1990).

10. Joseph Namath, *I Can't Wait until Tomorrow . . .'Cause I Get Better-Looking Every Day* (New York: Random House, 1969).

11. I am grateful to Jennifer Hochschild for drawing my attention to this.

12. Not all of those who heard the broadcast panicked. Were those who heard and did not believe in Martians less credulous or more faithful (to the conventional wisdom concerning Martians)? Were they better read—did they recognize the novel? Or were those who panicked distinguished by the fear that the imminent war in this world would be a war of unanticipated inhumanity, with weapons of unparalleled, if not unimagined, power? If there were those who read it so, they read it right.

13. James Fiskin's "deliberative opinion poll," proposed as part of a reconsideration of the electoral process, would mitigate (if not overcome) many of these difficulties. See his *Deliberation and Democracy* (New Haven: Yale University Press, 1991).

14. This reliance on the agreement of results as an indication of their truth is more frequently ascribed to the scientific character of the discipline. I do not dispute this, though practices in theoretical physics and mathematics suggest this should be qualified. I would note, however, mindful of Thomas Kuhn and over a generation of work on the cultural construction of science, that science, where it is understood in this fashion, relies equally upon this privileging of convention. See also Richard Rorty, "Science as Solidarity," in *Rhetoric and the Human Sciences* ed. John S. Nelson, Allan Megill, and Donald N. McCloskey, (Madison: University of Wisconsin Press, 1987).

15. It would show itself in other memorials as well. Judy Chicago's *Dinner Party* and the quilt emblazoned with the names of AIDS victims similarly commemorate the dead.

16. Louis Althusser, "Ideology and Ideological State Apparatuses," in *Lenin and Philosophy* (New York: Monthly Review Press, 1971), p. 174.

17. Ibid., p. 172.

18. Michel Foucault, "Afterword: The Subject and Power," in Herbert L. Dreyfus and Paul Rabinow, *Michel Foucault: Beyond Structuralism and Hermeneutics* (Chicago: University of Chicago Press, 1982), p. 216.

Chapter Two

1. I would like to have furnished the reader with these images but *Good Housekeeping* refused to grant permission for their use to the University of Chicago Press.

2. John Taylor of Caroline, *Arator* (from the 1818 edition; Indianapolis, Ind.: Liberty Classics, 1977), and Thomas Jefferson, *Notes on the State of Virginia,* and letters in Merrill Peterson, ed., *The Portable Thomas Jefferson* (New York: Viking Press, 1975). For John Randolph, see his speeches in Congress, some of which are collected in Russell Kirk, *John Randolph of Roanoke* (Chicago: Henry Regnery, 1964); Robert Dawidoff's excellent biography, *The Education of John Randolph* (New York: W. W. Norton, 1979); and my *Alternative Americas* (Chicago: University of Chicago Press, 1986), chap. 4.

3. The recognition of the semiotic function of goods is, of course, central to the literature of anthropology. It is also marked in works, from a variety of disciplines, on popular culture. These include Roland Barthes, *Mythologies* (New York: Hill and Wang, 1957); J. Baudrillard, *For a Critique of the Political Economy of the Sign,* trans. Charles Levin, (St. Louis, Mo.: Telos Press, 1981); Michel de Certeau, *The Practice of Everyday Life* (Berkeley: University of California Press, 1984); Mary Douglas and B. Isherwood, *The World of Goods: Towards an Anthropology of Consumption* (London: Allan Lane, 1979); John Fiske, *Reading the Popular* (Boston: Unwin Hyman, 1989), and *Understanding Popular Culture* (Boston: Unwin Hyman, 1989); Dick Hebdige, *Subculture: The Meaning of Style* (London: Methuen, 1979); J. Williamson, *Consuming Passions: The Dynamics of Popular Culture* (London: Marion Boyars, 1979); and Stuart Ewen, *All Consuming Images* (New York: Basic Books, 1988).

4. Judith Goldstein has written on the extended coverage of the excesses of Imelda Marcos and Michele Duvalier in the American press. She observes the differential treatment accorded to excessive consumption in women and in men and compares the collections of these women to those of traditional rulers. See Judith Goldstein, "Lifestyles of the Rich and Tyrannical," in *American Scholar,* Spring 1987, pp. 235–47.

5. See especially Melanie Klein, *Contributions to Psychoanalysis*

(London: Hogarth Press, 1948), and *Narrative of a Child Analysis* (New York: Delacorte Press, 1975); and C. G. Jung, *Four Archetypes,* Bollingen Series (Princeton: Princeton University Press, 1980).

6. This very brief discussion of Madonna is merely intended to acknowledge, and draw attention to, other writings on her. I am especially indebted to Ann Cvetkovich for many informal discussions of Madonna.

7. Susan Willis, "I Shop Therefore I Am: Is There a Place for African-American Culture in Commodity Culture?" in *Changing Our Own Words,* ed. Cheryl Wall (New Brunswick, N.J.: Rutgers University Press, 1989), pp. 177–78.

8. I do not mean to suggest that stereotypes of the black underclass are limited to a single slur, even on the score of criminality. An association of blacks with crimes against persons emerged in the 1960s in the wake of riots in Watts and Detroit. This association, which replaced the stereotype of the docile and obliging Uncle Tom, expressed metonymically the fear of (collective) black violence against whites. The practical effects of this metonymy become visible in the disparate treatment given whites and Asians involved in crimes of violence against blacks, and blacks involved in crimes of violence against whites and Asians. The speedy arrest of blacks accused of beating a white truck driver, Reginald Denny, in the Los Angeles riots of 1992 contrasted sharply with the legal absolution of the white police officers in the Rodney King case and the suspended sentence given a Korean grocer found guilty of manslaughter in the shooting of a young black man.

9. Stuart Hall, in a lecture at Princeton University in the spring of 1988, gave a brilliant account of the relations of center and periphery in the production and consumption of style. I have been unable to find this discussion in his published work, nor can I remember its nuances, but I should nevertheless like to acknowledge it here.

10. Thomas Dumm, "Lost in the Supermarket," unpublished essay, quoted by permission of the author. Dumm's essay considers the likeness of shopping to torture. This comparison, which Dumm himself presents as arbitrary, is warranted by the recognition that shopping and torture are both marked by the simultaneous evocation of subjectivity (in the privacy of pain and the exercise of choice) and its erasure (in pain as the negation of the conscious self and in the conversion of choice to compulsion). Both may also be understood as activities of articulation and dismemberment. The difference between them lies, as Dumm acknowledges, in the importance of pain.

11. Nuanced and amusing accounts of shopping as subversion are

provided in John Fiske's analyses of popular culture, particularly *Reading the Popular*, pp. 13–42.

12. See R. Bowlby, *Just Looking: Consumer Culture in Dreiser, Gissing, and Zola* (London: Methuen, 1985), p. 22, for another discussion and for an example of the recommendation of this strategy by Elizabeth Cady Stanton in the 1850s.

13. I have read several of these. I cite *The J. Peterman Company Owner's Manual No. 5,* from the J. Peterman Company, 2444 Palumbo Drive, Lexington, Ky. 40509.

14. Ibid., p. 5. The hat is also identified with the Canal Zone, "successfully bidding at Beaulieu," intimidation, and LBOs. Quite a hat. It might be argued against my reading that the J. Peterman Company also offers the "Coal Miner's Bag" and a mailbag. However, since the descriptive points of reference on color and texture and experience for these bags are such things as the leather seats of Jaguars, and driving home in a Bentley, I feel fairly confident in my reading.

15. Ibid., p. 3. See also pp. 15 and 17 for instance of women as the object of the male gaze. The identification of the gaze with male sexuality is unambiguous here as well.

16. Ibid., p. 17.

17. Ibid., pp. 7, 16, 20, 21, 37, and 50.

18. Ibid., p. 20.

19. Paul Smith, "Visiting the Banana Republic," in *Universal Abandon?* ed. Andrew Ross for Social Text (Minneapolis: University of Minnesota Press, 1988), pp. 128–48.

20. *The Nature Company Catalog,* the Nature Company, P.O. Box 2310, Berkeley, Calif. 94702, Spring 1990. See pp. 1–2 and order form insert between pp. 18 and 19. Note also the entailed donation to Designs for Conservation on p. 18.

21. This moment from the Home Shopping Network was generously brought to my attention, on videotape, by Peter Bregman, a student in my American Studies class of fall 1988, at Princeton University.

22. See Simon Schama, *The Embarrassment of Riches* (New York: Alfred A. Knopf, 1987).

23. *The Philosophy of Andy Warhol* (New York: Harcourt Brace Jovanovich, 1975).

24. For Warhol's interest in shopping, see *Philosophy of Andy Warhol.*

25. Susan Sontag, *Against Interpretation* (New York: Farrar, Strauss, Giroux, 1961), pp. 261, 265, and 268.

26. In our regard for representation. See Alexandre Kojeve, *Introduction to the Reading of Hegel* (New York: Basic Books, 1979).

27. Robert Coover, *The Public Burning* (New York: Viking Press, 1977), p. 7.

Chapter Three

1. In treating the President as sign, I call up a host of theoretical referents. The most conspicuous of these is Roland Barthes (Roland Barthes, *Mythologies,* trans. Annette Lavers [New York: Hill and Wang, 1972] pp. 109–59 and passim). It is Barthes's theory of signification that provides the account of the terms *sign, signifier,* and *signified* that I employ in this work, with two related and important qualifications. While I accept Barthes's contention that signs are intrinsically arbitrary, I do not believe that they remain so. Nor do I accept Barthes's contention that myth is always and everywhere to be condemned. While Barthes sees in mythologies "a nauseating mixture of common opinions," Nietzsche regards myth as a necessary redemption from Dionysiac nausea. "Every culture that has lost myth has lost its natural healthy creativity. Only a horizon ringed about with myths can unify a culture" (Friedrich Nietzsche, *The Birth of Tragedy* [New York: Doubleday, 1956], pp. 51–52 and 137). Althusser's contention that, in language, there is no escape from ideology is also relevant here. I argue, with Althusser, that ideologies are embedded in language and, with Rousseau, that men are, in language, embedded in ideologies; "different languages make different men" (Jean-Jacques Rousseau, *Emile, or On Education,* trans. Allan Bloom [New York: Basic Books, 1979], p. 109). I argue, with Nietzsche, and with Freud, that myths are essential to a culture's integrity. *Myth* should connote neither derogation nor condemnation.

2. Alexis de Tocqueville, *Democracy in America,* trans. George Lawrence (New York: Doubleday, 1969), p. 135.

3. Those who believe (I confess I do not) the results of those surveys that suggest that a majority of voters are ignorant of (or mistaken in) the stands taken by the candidate of their choice must be still more skeptical of the claim that election represents the triumph of a doctrine in the minds of a majority of the nation.

4. Vachel Lindsay, "Bryan, Bryan, Bryan," in *Selected Poems of Vachel Lindsay,* ed. Mark Harris (New York: Macmillan, 1963).

5. *Mythologies,* p. 117.

6. Ibid., p. 118.

7. Note that Barthes is at some pains (in *Mythologies,* though not

consistently so elsewhere) to deny or depreciate this possibility of subversion.

8. See Ernst Kantorowicz, *The King's Two Bodies,* (Princeton: Princeton University Press, 1957). This extraordinarily rich study has inspired a series of fine works, including Michael Rogin, "The King's Two Bodies," in *Public Values and Private Power in American Politics,* ed. David Greenstone (Chicago: University of Chicago Press, 1982), pp. 71–103, and *Zone,* ed. Michael Feher, Ramona Naddaff, and Nadia Tazi (New York: Urzone, 1989), 1, 2, and 3 on the body.

9. Primarily Ronald Reagan with Richard Hubler, *Where's the Rest of Me?* (New York: Duell, Sloan and Pearce, 1965).

10. Reagan and Hubler, *Where's the Rest of Me?* p. 1.

11. *Time,* February 23, 1981, p. 12.

12. Michael Rogin, *Fathers and Children* (New York: Alfred A. Knopf, 1978).

13. Vachel Lindsay, "The Statue of Old Andrew Jackson," in *Selected Poems of Vachel Lindsay,* p. 129.

14. Lloyd de Mause, *Reagan's America* (New York: Creative Books, 1984), p. 95. Freudian theory argues, unconsciously, for a Keynesian interpretation. The end product is not debt but money.

15. William Greider, "The Education of David Stockman," *Atlantic Monthly,* December 1981, p. 51.

16. Ibid.

17. Ibid., p. 40.

18. Reagan, quoted in *New York Times,* December 11, 1983, p. 1.

19. Reagan and Hubler, *Where's the Rest of Me?* p. 118.

20. Ibid., pp. 118–19.

21. Jack Smith, *Los Angeles Times,* May 22, 1985.

22. *New York Post,* April 29, 1981, p. 2.

23. Fred Somkin, *Unquiet Eagle* (Ithaca, N.Y.: Cornell University Press, 1967), p. 45.

24. Hugh Gallagher, *FDR's Splendid Deception* (New York: Dodd, Mead, 1985), pp. xiii-xiv.

25. See for Example: Noel Busch, *What Manner of Man?* (New York: Harper Bros., 1944); and John Flynn, *The Roosevelt Myth* (New York: Devin, Adair, 1945).

26. Vernon Quinn, *Picture Story of Franklin D. Roosevelt* (New York: Frederick A. Stokes, 1934), pp. 25–28.

27. Gallagher, *FDR's Splendid Deception,* 96.

28. James MacGregor Burns, *Roosevelt: The Lion and the Fox* (New York: Harcourt, Brace and World, 1956). See also Harold Gosnell, *Champion Campaigner: Franklin D. Roosevelt* (New York: Macmillan, 1952).

29. Philip Hambruger in the *New Yorker,* quoted in Gallagher, *FDR's Splendid Deception,* p. 79.

30. Ibid., p. 61.

31. Ibid.

32. Ibid, p. 74; and Burns, *Roosevelt,* p. 103.

33. Flynn, *Roosevelt Myth,* p. 5. This is particularly true in the case of Franklin Roosevelt's relative and predecessor in office, Theodore Roosevelt.

34. *Time,* January 5, 1942.

35. Gallagher, *FDR's Splendid Deception,* 96.

36. Robert MacElvaine, *Letters from the Forgotten Man: Down and Out in the Great Depression* (Chapel Hill: University of North Carolina Press, 1982).

37. Gallagher, *FDR's Splendid Deception,* p. 74. See also MacElvaine, *Letters from the Forgotten Man,* 106:

Roosevelt's paralysis was absolutely critical to Roosevelt's later relationship with victims of the Great Depression. It worked both ways. He was able to understand suffering in a way a country gentleman would not otherwise have been likely to. And, to the deprived, the smiling "the only thing we have to fear is fear itself" attitude Roosevelt took in the face of the Depression was acceptable and uplifting only because he had overcome a terrible affliction himself.

38. MacElvaine, *Letters from the Forgotten Man,* p. 48.

39. *New York World,* June 28, 1928.

40. Alfred Jones, *Roosevelt's Image Brokers* (Kennikat: National University Publications, 1974), p. 70.

41. MacElvaine, *Letters from the Forgotten Man,* pp. 215, 219, and 220.

42. Vachel Lindsay, "Abraham Lincoln Walks at Midnight," *Selected Poems of Vachel Lindsay,* p. 129.

43. MacElvaine, *Letters from the Forgotten Man,* p. 208.

44. Jones, *Roosevelt's Image Brokers,* p. 71.

45. Nancy Weiss, *Farewell to the Party of Lincoln* (Princeton: Princeton University Press, 1983), p. 225.

46. Jones, *Roosevelt's Image Brokers,* p. 71.

47. Ibid., p. 76.

48. Ibid., p. 72.

49. Ibid., p. 70.

50. Ibid., p. 93.

51. Carl Sandburg, "Lincoln-Roosevelt," *Today,* February 10, 1934, quoted that time had worked great changes in Lincoln, who opposed labor activities in his own time.

52. Shown at the 1984 Republican National Convention. As Jeffrey Tulis pointed out to me, the commemorative coins of the 1984 Olympics, issued by the U.S. Olympic Committee, show figures with a curiously apposite defect; they have no heads.

53. Jeffrey Tulis, *The Rhetorical Presidency* (Princeton: Princeton University Press, 1988).

54. Michael Oreskes, "What Poison Politics Has Done to America," *New York Times,* Sunday, October 29, 1989, sec. 4, p. 1.

55. John Fiske argues that one of the popular pleasures of television is the recognition that one can see without being seen: the enjoyment of surveillance over others, of one's own exemption from surveillance (*Reading the Popular*). I believe this overrates the quotidian experience of television as a means of surveillance and underrates the use of television as a means for the display of power to the less powerful and the powerless.

56. Michael Rogin provides a revealing analysis of Nixon's experience of subjection in "The King's Two Bodies" (in *Ronald Reagan, The Movie* [Berkeley: University of California Press, 1987], pp. 81–114). Nixon, Rogin observes, conflated his body personal with the body politic. His visceral sense of surveillance is perhaps best captured in a response he made to a question during a televised interview with David Frost. When asked if being subjected to scrutiny as President was like being under a microscope, Nixon responded that the experience more nearly resembled a proctoscopy.

57. There have been a few cases in which television refused a presidential request for access. These are so rare, however, that they are news in themselves.

Chapter Four

1. See Jean-Jacques Rousseau, *On the Social Contract,* trans. Judith Masters, ed. Roger Masters (New York: St. Martin's Press, 1978), and *Emile, or On Education.*

2. See Jacques Lacan, *Ecrits,* trans. Alan Sheridan (New York: W. W. Norton, 1977), and *Four Fundamental Concepts of Psychoanalysis,* trans. Alan Sheridan (New York: W. W. Norton, 1978);

Plato, *Symposium,* Loeb Edition, trans. W. R. M. Lamb (Cambridge: Harvard University Press, 1975).

3. The recognition of the authority of language shows itself throughout modern philosophy in the works of Nietzsche, Martin Heidegger, Ludwig Wittgenstein, Leo Strauss, Hans Georg Gadamer, Jacques Derrida, Michel Foucault, J. L. Austen, and innumerable others. It animates debates over texts, textuality, and the status and the standards of interpretation. The preeminence of these questions among such diverse thinkers recalls Nietzsche's statement (*On the Genealogy of Morals* trans. Walter Kaufmann and R. J. Hollingdale (New York: Random House, 1969) that we are all philologists now.

4. George Steiner, "Our Homeland, the Text."

5. The relation of pornography to representation was brought to my attention by many very valued conversations with Donald Downs.

6. This should inflect, but cannot decide, the debate over pornography. The parties to this debate should, and generally do, avoid equating representations with the acts they represent. (This question is, of course, distinct from questions concerning how the representation was produced.) This does not, however, render such images ethically neutral. The recognition that representation is the medium through which we constitute as well as express political identities obliges one to subject representations to scrutiny.

7. Richard Flathman, in a talk at the University of Texas in February of 1990, observed that those who will must remain ignorant of the outcome of their willing, indeed, even of its content in the fullest sense. Will, in itself and in its action, is aporetic.

8. See Nietzsche, *On the Genealogy of Morals,* 2:1–5. Promises require transubstantiation. The capacity to promise, and perhaps the promises themselves, must be written on one's body.

9. Luigi Barzini, *The Europeans* (New York: Simon and Schuster, 1983), p. 136.

10. Sotirios Barber captures the "aspirational" character of the Constitution and elaborates the consequences of this view with clarity and force in *What the Constitution Means* (Baltimore: Johns Hopkins University Press, 1984).

11. The placement of the founding, whether at the moment (difficult to ascertain) of the Constitution's writing or that of its ratification, and the consequent identification of the founders, are issues of great moment for the partisans of this view, and ones that, were they to examine the issues, present them with a set of revealing questions. Their failure to confront these questions is equally revealing.

12. Early examples of this can be found in the writings of prominent antislavery activists (notably William Garrison) and feminists. It is interesting to observe that the strategy of diminishing the founders (rather than elevating the authority of the people) resurfaced in the 1960s among some civil rights and feminist activists, and that it has provoked the same response of mindless adulation among some conservatives. The peculiar symmetry of these strategies of mummification and muckraking, and the consequent ease of debate between the two parties, have perpetuated both strategies far longer than their intellectual merits warrant.

185

13. Jurgen Habermas, *Legitimation Crisis,* trans. Thomas McCarthy (Boston: Beacon Press, 1975).

14. This phrase is a translation of the name given to their actions by reformers in Japan during the Tokugawa period. I am indebted to Tetsuo Najita and Harry Harootunian for making me aware of it.

15. The Koran begins with the command to speech, "Recite." It is addressed to both the prophet and the faithful and thus, like the present tense in which the Constitution is written, puts the reader in the place of the founder. In Genesis the world is spoken into being.

Chapter Five

1. Robert Ferguson, *Law and Letters in American Culture* (Cambridge: Harvard University Press, 1984), p. 11. Ferguson's work is admirable not only for the strength of his arguments for the centrality of the law in America but for his recognition of the law as at once an instance of and an alternative to literature.

2. Ibid.

3. Thomas Carter, quoted in Diane Holloway, "Justice to Be Served Wednesday," *Austin American-Statesman,* Sunday, January 6, 1991.

4. Public Enemy, "Louder Than a Bomb," "Prophets of Rage," and "Party for Your Right to Fight," *It Takes a Nation of Millions to Hold Us Back,* Ridenhour, Shocklee, and Sadler.

5. Walt Whitman, "States!" in *Walt Whitman: The Complete Poems,* ed. Francis Murphy (New York: Penguin Books, 1975), pp. 219 and 620.

6. Though "I grew up in a house with the television always on," I have to acknowledge the help of Brian Downing and Deborah Harrold in preparing this list.

7. This is a theme central to what Sacvan Bercovitch calls *The American Jeremiad* (Madison: University of Wisconsin Press, 1978). It sounded with particular clarity in Martin Luther King's coupling of

civil disobedience with the declaration "We will not be satisfied until justice rolls down like water, and righteousness like a mighty stream."

8. I am indebted to Deborah Harrold for pointing out to me that the institutional structures of the judicial system in Britain and its American colony once spoke against the identification of substantive with procedural justice. The division of courts of law and courts of equity marked a division between law and justice. The observation, readily arrived at by those with common sense or a mature experience of the world, that the law does not always secure justice was recorded and preserved in the presence of courts of equity. These served an appropriately dual purpose. The presence of courts of equity provided a means for securing justice where precedent and abstraction might produce a legal, but nonetheless unjust, outcome. This presence also marked the limits of abstraction, presenting a structural reminder that procedural rigor is not identical to the end it is nominally intended to serve.

9. Kim Lane Scheppele, "Constitutionalizing the Interpretation of Social Practise," paper presented at the annual meeting of the American Political Science Association, 1987, p. 3. In this paper, Scheppele gives a detailed description of the process of constructing—and deconstructing—the facts in a particular case. For an elaboration of the argument presented in this paper see chapter 5 of Kim Lane Scheppele, *Legal Secrets: Equality and Efficiency in the Common Law* (Chicago: University of Chicago Press, 1988).

10. Ibid.

11. Ibid., pp. 5–6.

12. I am (once again) obliged to Deborah Harrold for the argument concerning the important contradiction constitutive of the jury system. Having experienced myself the unusual ire most lawyers feel when confronted with this demystification, incriminating her as its author almost seems a poor return for so fine an insight. I am also grateful to Sanford Levinson, who confirmed this heretical view and furnished several examples of explicit acknowledgments of the jury's ambivalent relation to the law.

13. ART. 2, Sec. 9 secures "the privilege of the Writ of Habeas Corpus" against suspension. ART. 3, Sec. 2 states that "the trial of all Crimes, except in Cases of Impeachment, shall be by Jury."

14. Jean-Jacques Rousseau, *Du contrat social*, ed. Roger Grimsley (Oxford: Oxford University Press, 1972), p. 187, my translation.

15. The citizen's authority is not, however, wholly absent. The citizen on trial is engaged in the making of law as a participant in a collective enterprise. The trial in which the citizen is involved, as subject,

will enter into the legal records to challenge or buttress the law. The citizen also, of course, participates in the determination of law through the courts as sovereign, and hence as a participant in the actions and influence of those who represent the state.

16. Derrida, *Of Grammatology,* p. 134.

Chapter Six

1. In the Gettysburg Address. "Fourscore and seven years ago, our fathers brought forth upon this continent a new nation."

2. In the Preamble. "We the People of the United States of America . . . do ordain and establish this Constitution." The recognition of the ambivalent textuality of the Constitution has produced a diverse and illuminating literature in public law and constitutional studies. Among those accounts that speak to the point I raise here are William Harris, "Bonding Word and Polity," *American Political Science Review,* March 1982, pp. 34–45; and my article "Transubstantiation: The Dialectic of Constitutional Authority," *University of Chicago Law Review,* Spring 1987, pp. 458–72. Sotirios Barber and Sanford Levinson have written widely and well on this and related questions. I am grateful to them, and to Will Harris, Ellen Kennedy, Cass Sunstein, Kim Scheppele, and Bruce Ackerman, for enabling me to see the intellectual power and the unanswered questions of the Constitution.

3. The evident embodiment of speech may be the decisive element in establishing its primacy in liberalism. Self-preservation for all liberals, assembly for Rousseau, the establishment of original property, and the possession of rights for Locke all link liberalism to the privileging of embodiment.

4. Derrida, *Of Grammatology,* p. 134.

5. Rousseau's works contain an extraordinarily complex and interesting economy of speech and writing. Derrida supplies an account of Rousseau and writing in *Of Grammatology.* Look, too, to Rousseau's analysis of writing in *On the Origin of Languages,* trans. John Moran (Chicago: University of Chicago Press, 1966). In distinguishing the phonetic alphabet from ideograms and hieroglyphics, Rousseau notes its connection to a particular political economy—one of trade and representation. The demands of trade require the trader to learn multiple languages. The need to represent the sounds of other languages is said to produce the phonetic alphabet. The phonetic alphabet functions as money does, permitting exchange (of words, of goods) through a system of representation that renders the exchanged commensurable.

This alphabet is also manifestly deconstructive; it breaks down the representational media of speech for analysis. It casts speech into writing. The connection between the spoken and the written in ideograms and hieroglyphs is more arbitrary and less intimate than in the phonetic alphabet.

6. The bulk of these criticisms has been directed toward Jacques Derrida and Michel Foucault. This insight into the determinative power of language is not, of course, peculiar to them. An interesting, somewhat eccentric, argument for the priority of writing over—and in—speech can be found in Elias Canetti, *Crowds and Power*, trans. Carol Stewart (New York: Farrar, Strauss, Giroux, 1984). The argument for the presence of writing in speech is presented as well by Paul Ricoeur in his excellent essay "The Model of the Text: Cultural Considered as a Text" (in Paul Rabinow and William Sullivan, eds., *Interpretive Social Science: A Reader* [Berkeley: University of California Press], 1979, pp. 73–102), by Hans Georg Gadamer (see especially "Man and Language," in *Philosophical Hermeneutics*, ed. David Linge [Berkeley: University of California Press, 1976]), and by Lacan (see *Ecrits*).

7. Richard Flathman is a notable exception and conscious of himself as such. See *Toward a Liberalism* (Ithaca, N.Y.: Cornell University Press, 1989).

8. The text may be usefully understood as that "veil of ignorance" that intervenes between the mythic subject of John Rawls's account and the world to be made. It appears neutral, yet it imposes features on the subject. John Rawls, *A Theory of Justice* (Cambridge: Harvard University Press, 1971).

9. See Sigmund Freud, *Group Psychology and the Analysis of the Ego* (New York: W. W. Norton, 1959), p. 1 and passim.

10. It lacked. As I argue, following Lacan and Melanie Klein, in *Reflections on Political Identity* (Baltimore: Johns Hopkins University Press, 1988), it was only because of lack that it existed at all.

11. Foucault, "Afterword," p. 216.

12. This has been reiterated in academic works and the popular press. The charge, commonly directed at Jacques Derrida, Michel Foucault, and J. Baudrillard, also embraces Nietzsche, whose early recognition of our constitution and consequent admonition "we are all philologists now" instructed hermeneuticists and poststructuralists. Nietzsche was, those so inclined declare, not a philosopher but a poet. One of Foucault's most useful contributions has been to remind us to look critically at the covert politics of disciplinary demarcation.

13. For examples of such assumptions see Bruce Ackerman, *Social Justice and the Liberal State* (New Haven: Yale University Press,

1980); and Rogers Smith, "Political Jurisprudence, the 'New Institutionalism,' and Public Law," in *American Political Science Review,* March 1988, pp. 89–108. I am very much indebted to both these men for their clear, compelling, and determined presentations of this position, in writing and in conversation.

14. A variety of inscriptive strategies have been articulated by scholars of race and gender. Denigration has been deconstructed etymologically. The erasure of women was read first, and most literally, in *mankind* and *man,* and in references to the (nominally ungendered) individual as *he.* The denigration of people of color was read, again quite literally, in the dictionary, where *black* conveyed not merely a color or a race but evil and ugliness. Later scholars extended this analysis to more subtle inscriptions. I have been particularly impressed by Carole Pateman's discussion of the gender of the liberal individual in *The Sexual Contract* (Palo Alto: Stanford University Press, 1988); Luce Irigaray's *The Sex Which Is Not One,* trans. Catherine Porter (Ithaca, N.Y.: Cornell University Press, 1985), and *Speculum of the Other Woman,* trans. Gillian Gill (Ithaca, N.Y.: Cornell University Press, 1985); Judith Butler's *Gender Trouble* (New York: Routledge, 1990); and Homi Bhabha's "Of Mimicry and Man," *October* 34 (Fall 1985): 71–80, and "Sly Civility," *October* 28 (Spring 1984): 125–33.

15. I am indebted to Michael Rogin for drawing my attention to blackface. His careful, nuanced reading of the images in *The Jazz Singer* brilliantly exposes the erasure of blacks in the assumptions of blackface.

16. Barthes, *Mythologies,* pp. 146–48.

17. Eric Hobsbawm, *Bandits* (New York: Pantheon, 1969).

18. E. H. Gombrich, "The Edge of Delusion," a review of David Freedberg's *The Power of Images,* in the *New York Review of Books,* February 15, 1990, p. 6.

19. Ibid.

20. On separation see Jacques Lacan, *The Four Fundamental Concepts of Psychoanalysis,* trans. Alan Sheridan, ed. Jacques-Alain Miller (New York: W. W. Norton, 1981), p. 214; Anne Norton, *Reflections on Political Identity* (Baltimore: Johns Hopkins University Press, 1988), pp. 11–26.

21. Derrida, *Of Grammatology,* p. 145.

22. Doubly difficult. It is difficult, given the terms of debate we presently employ—the rules of the game—to detach that message analytically and show it for what it is. It is no less difficult to divest that image of that meaning, to use it in a way that will not convey the racist constructions attached to it.

23. Examples of Eddie Murphy as Buckwheat, as the proprietor of the Velvet Jones School of Technology ("Be a Ho"), and as Mr. Robinson ("Mr. Robinson's Neighborhood") can be found on *Saturday Night Live: The Best of Eddie Murphy.*

24. Max Weber, "The Meaning of Ethical Neutrality," in *Methodology of the Social Sciences,* trans. Edward Shils and Henry Finch (New York: Free Press, 1949), p. 8.

25. Consider traditional feminine dress. Women who adopted the dress of men—or, like Amelia Bloomer, modified it—challenged the limits written in dress. Women, like Madonna, who exaggerated elements of traditional feminine dress mocked the traditional identities it had once affirmed.